my poems
won't change
the world

A BILINGUAL EDITION
WITH TRANSLATIONS BY

gini alhadeff

judith baumel

geoffrey brock

moira egan and damiano abeni

jonathan galassi

jorie graham

kenneth koch

j. d. mcclatchy

david shapiro

susan stewart and brunella antomarini

mark strand

rosanna warren

patrizia
cavalli

my poems
won't change
the world

selected
poems

edited by
gini alhadeff

FARRAR STRAUS GIROUX

NEW YORK

Farrar, Straus and Giroux
18 West 18th Street, New York 10011

Printed in the United States of America
First edition, 2013

These poems originally appeared in Italian in the following publications:
  Le mie poesie non cambieranno il mondo (My Poems Won't Change the World) © 1974
Giulio Einaudi Editore, s.p.a., Torino.
  Il cielo (The Sky) © 1981 Giulio Einaudi Editore, s.p.a., Torino.
  L'io singolare proprio mio (The All Mine Singular I), from *Poesie (1974–1992)*
© 1992, 2007 Giulio Einaudi Editore, s.p.a., Torino.
  Sempre aperto teatro (Forever Open Theater) (1999) © 1999, 2006 Giulio Einaudi
Editore, s.p.a., Torino.
  Pigre divinità e pigra sorte (Lazy Gods, Lazy Fate) (2006) © 2006, 2007 Giulio
Einaudi Editore, s.p.a., Torino.

Owing to limitations of space, acknowledgments for permission to print previously
published and unpublished material can be found on pages 275–77.

Library of Congress Cataloging-in-Publication Data
Cavalli, Patrizia, 1947–
    [Poems. English. Selections]
    My poems won't change the world : selected poems / Patrizia Cavalli ;
  [introduction, translation, and] edited by Gini Alhadeff. — First edition.
      pages cm
    Text in English and Italian.
    Includes index.
    ISBN 978-0-374-21744-0
    1. Cavalli, Patrizia, 1947—Translations into English. I. Alhadeff, Gini.
  II. Title. III. Title: My poems will not change the world.

  PQ4863.A8894A235 2013
  851'.914—dc23

                                                        2013014362

Designed by Quemadura

www.fsgbooks.com
www.twitter.com/fsgbooks
www.facebook.com/fsgbooks

10 9 8 7 6 5 4 3 2 1

contents

FROM Il cielo
The Sky (1981)

Ah sì, per tua disgrazia
Ah yes, to your misfortune

Quando si è colti all'improvviso da salute
When one finds one's self unexpectedly selected by health

Non giochi più, mangi soltanto
You no longer play, you only eat

Mangiava una mela Macintosh
Eating a Macintosh apple

Mi ero tagliata i capelli, scurite le sopracciglia
I had cut my hair, darkened my eyebrows

Adesso che il tempo sembra tutto mio
Now that time seems all mine

Così arrivi, come sempre
You arrive like this, as always

Che la morte mi avvenga dentro un desiderio
Let death come to me wrapped in a wish

È inutile fare sforzi
There's no point in trying

Come se fosse una spanatura
As though out of register

introduction

An early collection of Patrizia Cavalli's poems, *Il cielo* (1974), is dedicated to Okapi Bandierina, a cat sired by Caruso Mandulino who came from the house of the great Italian novelist Elsa Morante. Caruso and his consort, Carulina, had one hundred and eighty kittens with which Morante kept her friends supplied over the years. I live in Manhattan with an Italian writer and anthropologist who grew up with a succession of those cats—three in all. His parents would drive out to the beach with Morante and her husband Alberto Moravia, and the two famously fought all the way there and back. But the cats—the soulful Romeo, then Useppe, who died young and was so called because he was the son of Giuseppe, and finally, Zapyron—were placid stubtailed Siamese. By the time Patrizia met Morante and they became friends, Moravia was gone, though the cats remained. Having come from Todi in the late '60s to major in philosophy, Patrizia knew no one in Rome but was somehow taken up by a group of talented Americans who thought her very funny, though she didn't speak a word of English at the time. It was one of them, a musician, who introduced her to Elsa Morante. On most days at midday Patrizia would collect Elsa in her Fiat Cinquecento and they would go to a different trattoria for lunch, then they'd hang around cafés with a changing cast of friends till about four, when Elsa would go home, unhook the phone, disconnect the doorbell, take a little bite of amphetamine, and settle down to work for the remainder of the day, often late into the night. (She was writing her masterpiece, *La storia*, at the time.) After they'd known each other for two years, as they were leaving the old Roman restaurant Campana and heading towards the Piazza Navona, Elsa stopped and, almost pinning Patrizia to a wall, asked, "What is it you do, anyway?" Patrizia muttered, "Well, I write poems." Elsa demanded to see them. After several months, and repeated promptings by Morante, Patrizia complied. An hour later Morante called to say, "I am really glad, Patrizia: you're a poet." To Patrizia it meant that she would remain in the orbit of her friend. That first collection, from which this one borrows its title, *Le mie poesie non cambieranno il mondo* (My Poems Won't Change the World), published in 1974, was dedicated to Elsa.

I met Patrizia Cavalli in 2006, and a month later received in the mail a copy of *Pigre divinità e pigra sorte* (Lazy Gods, Lazy Fate), her latest collection. The title page was inscribed in Patrizia's neat and barely legible handwriting in which the tall t's are the most conspicuous element. A cat we had back in 2006 immediately pierced all four corners of the cover with repeated tooth marks, and I liked the poems so much I spontaneously started to translate them. I write in both Italian and English, so I did it by ear. "It wasn't science, it was devotion," goes one line in "The Keeper" ("La guardiana"), the longest poem in this collection, almost a novella of stinting love, technically described, in verse. I had begun, indolently, with one of the shortest:

> Here I am, I do my bit,
> though I don't know what that may be.
> If I did I could at least let go of it
> and free of it be free of being me.

More than half of this book, however, is made up of poems from Patrizia's previous collections published by Einaudi, from 1974 to 1999, and now freshly translated by an illustrious group of American poets, most of them already familiar with Patrizia's work. Mark

Strand, Jorie Graham, and Jonathan Galassi tackled up to a dozen; Rosanna Warren four thorny ones; Geoffrey Brock a few more; Sandy McClatchy and David Shapiro a few less. As their translations began to arrive, they were sometimes accompanied by comments on what it had been like to translate "Patrizia's music," as Jorie Graham termed it, into American English. Graham added, "They are not at all as simple to do as it seems—one wants to make them flow in this other language. There is a rate of speed that English will render as almost a platitude. I have tried to retain the richness of multiple meanings over the speed of transfer. And Cavalli's Italian is so effortlessly, naturally idiomatic, and idiom is clipped, whereas in American English we would have to choose a specific idiom, and that risks sounding totally phony and betraying their easy universality of tone. So I am privileging voice and speed of image, and also, as much as possible, trying to replicate in some manner their sonic properties—even if it is with *other* sonic properties. Of course in Italian, as we all know, everything rhymes with everything!"

Geoffrey Brock wrote: "I like to try to give her poems a loose metrical backbone in English that is (more or less) analogous to her use of meter in Italian, which I've always found pleasing and striking. I also try to use rhyme in similar ways, where possible, especially where the effect of a particular poem depends on it to a significant degree. One of the things I love about her poems in Italian is the way her contemporary voice so often makes use of and thereby revitalizes certain traditional techniques, and since that's something I think about a lot in relation to my own work, it naturally becomes part of my interest in hers."

Rosanna Warren said: "My approach was to use a flexible English pentameter as a base for three of these, because Patrizia uses a flexible hendecasyllable meter. I find these poems fascinating in their combination of colloquial, casual diction; Petrarchan philosophical diction (*il mio bene, il mio male*); very direct, prosaic statements; occasional liftoff into figurative language; a general curtness and rapidity of thought. That at least was what I was trying to catch in English."

In the middle of translating twelve of the most "daunting" of Cavalli's poems, "Affresco della notte palombara" ("Fresco of the underwater night"), Jonathan Galassi, who has translated Montale and Leopardi, wrote, "This is fun!" Some reminded him of Montale, and one in particular, "Com'era dolce ieri immaginarmi un albero!" ("How sweet it was yesterday imagining I was a tree!") seemed to echo precisely Montale's poem "L'agave sullo scoglio."

David Shapiro said, "It's what any good analyst wants—she is giving you the *état présent* of her entire soul, her present state, and the world's present. One poem equals her world." When we finished translating, "I became good. And like a goody-goody" (p. 237), he said, "It's very violent, like early Cézanne." And of the verses below that, "If you discovered a Greek poem and it was like this people would be very happy."

> Love was winning me over
> it didn't win my strength
> because I wasn't strong
> I was weak, defeated.
> Love gripped me
> it might have been strong
> but it wasn't, wasn't
> strong love, but
> lordly.

A dangerous moment in the chronicles of translation came when, to demonstrate the line "mi tuffavo / tra quei cuscini" ("I'd plunge into the cushions") to Mark Strand, Patrizia took a nosedive into a sofa—and that was with a fresh wrist injury. She was quite certain that the ghosts of a hallowed institution to which she had been invited as resident poet had taken offense at her strictures—mostly directed at the food served there—and dashed her to the ground as she gingerly attempted to step out of her elegant custom-made French trousers one night.

> A narcissist no more, vanity gone,
> what's left? A mix of waiting
> and headaches. Thoughts fail me,
> I drag my feet, my latest sin,
> sanctity.

On the subject of sanctity, in Rome one night I had an implacable migraine—I'd been in bed unable to eat or drink—and Patrizia arrived, with her swaggering step, hair cut so one side comes down along the line of her jaw in a curving point, like a sickle, and gave me an injection that made it all go away. She, too, suffers from terrible headaches, and most of the time from a multitude of ills that others, like Gulliver, might experience as the pricking of fine pins, but which to her are nails gruesomely planted in her psyche. If a wrist is damaged in a fall, as it was that day, every shocking blast and twinge of pain will travel to her brain on a vociferous stream of possible catastrophic consequences announcing themselves in unequivocal terms. Her mental rumblings—psychology—are as loud as her physical ones—physiology—and demand equal amounts of attention. In so many of her poems the body plays a leading role—the amorous, and always the thinking body—a body perceiving itself through eye and fingertip, heart, vagus nerve, lymph node, all with pens at their disposal. (Patrizia writes longhand.) In the Palazzo Doria Pamphilj apartment of her friends Isabella and Vicky Ducrot, Patrizia played me a song by a young Italian composer for which she had written the lyrics. When the music stopped, she said furtively, "It's about masturbation—could you tell?" "Yes," I lied. To a reporter of the daily *L'Unità* who'd asked whether it was true that she was her own favorite subject, she said, in 2002: "I have no special predilection for Patrizia Cavalli. I am nothing but an object of inquiry that provokes certain feelings and considerations in me as others might. The difference is that being in my own way day and night, I have become rather an expert knower of myself and it could be that a certain fondness has developed. That's all. And seeing that I'm from Umbria, if I'd been born in the thirteenth century I might have been a famous mystic." The Italian philosopher Giorgio Agamben said of her that she has written "the most intensely 'ethical' poetry in Italian literature of the twentieth century"; one could add that it is, easily, also the most sensual and comical.

I saw a table Patrizia laid out one Christmas. The tablecloth was white with little red stars. There were lilac and white hyacinths, and white tulips. Pomegranates and lemons and quince and persimmons. Two types of nougat, light and dark, a green plastic frog, its mouth open. An angel and three shepherdesses. A dark stone and an oblong one the color of sparkling amber. A raised round dish of tangerines. Some tropical fruit in dark spiny husks. Mark Strand has often sat at Patrizia's long wide table at her apartment on Via del Biscione, where to go from room to room one must climb up two steps, down three, with uneven walls and corners, and terra-cotta-tiled floors, beamed ceilings and a small terrace off the studio. That table tends to be covered with delicacies and the sort of wine so exquisite and ruinously expensive one gasps when Patrizia announces the price of a bottle, which she likes to do. Her money comes from poetry, though once upon a time she used to play poker and sell paintings on the side (or the other way around), and from her translations of Shakespeare's *A Midsummer Night's Dream* and *The Tempest*, which draw sustained crowds all over Italy whenever they are performed. Any hall she has ever read her poetry in, such as Renzo Piano's new Auditorium, or the immense remains of the Basilica of Maxentius, is invariably filled to the gills. Women like her, girls like her, and men like her, too. In Rome, and not just in her immediate neighborhood, the butcher, the baker, the bookseller, and several of the vendors at the vegetable stands on Campo dei Fiori call to Patrizia by her first name, actually a Roman version of it, as in, "Ah Patrí." The reason for this is that she chooses ingredients with the same somnambulistic precision with which she chooses words, and this entails long conversations as to where a certain Roman zucchini with ridges might have been grown, or at which mountain farm an egg might have been hatched. One summer in Rome, I told Patrizia that I had encountered a ricotta with a wonderful taste of sheep's milk and she said, a bit sternly—she is mostly stern on the subject of food—that ricotta should taste of innocence. I started buying it from a different store on Via della Croce when I understood what she meant. Patrizia is interested in innocence. You could say it is her main subject and preoccupation and one thing, when she glimpses it, that gives her pleasure. She let me translate her. I understood after a bit that it is one of the tortures a poet submits to, a slightly preferable one to not being translated. A cat may look at a king, my grandmother used to say, and anyone can translate anybody they choose. But it could be that while Patrizia was deciding where to have lunch on a certain day in Rome with Elsa Morante, I was somehow becoming worthy of my present predicament: in a somber Florentine boarding school I translated pink poems by Allen Ginsberg, and green and blue harangues by Jerry Rubin and Eldridge Cleaver that came for me in Mitsouko-scented envelopes from Fernanda Pivano, for her psychedelic and pacifist literary magazine *Pianeta Fresco*. Following in the footsteps of Cesare Pavese, her mentor, Pivano had taken on the task of bringing contemporary American literature, from Hemingway to the Beat poets (and much later the Minimalists) to Italy. I know I am not betraying her trust by helping to bring one lucidly beating heart of our current Italian literature to America. In Italy, Patrizia is as beloved as Wisława Szymborska still is in Poland, and if Italy were Japan she'd be designated a national treasure. Anthologies of her poems have been published in Germany, France, and Spain. It's time we had an American version of "Patrizia's music."

gini alhadeff

my poems
won't change
the world

from

le mie poesie
non cambieranno
il mondo 1974

A ELSA

from

my poems won't change the world 1974

TO ELSA

Qualcuno mi ha detto
che certo le mie poesie
non cambieranno il mondo.

Io rispondo che certo sì
le mie poesie
non cambieranno il mondo.

Someone told me
of course my poems
won't change the world.

I say yes of course
my poems
won't change the world.

GINI ALHADEFF

Eternità e morte insieme mi minacciano:
nessuna delle due conosco,
nessuna delle due conoscerò.

Together eternity and death threaten me:
neither of the two do I know,
neither of the two will I know.

JUDITH BAUMEL

Per riposarmi
mi pettino i capelli,
chi ha fatto ha fatto
e chi non ha fatto farà.

Dietro la bottiglia
i baffi della gatta,
le referenze
le darò domani.

Ora mi specchio
e mi metto il cappello,
aspetto visite aspetto
il suono del campanello.

Occhi bruni belli e addormentati . . .

Ma d'amore
non voglio parlare,
l'amore lo voglio
solamente fare.

I comb my hair
to unwind,
ready or not
here I am.

Behind the bottle
the cat's whiskers,
I'll send off those
references later.

I put on a hat,
look in the mirror,
I'm expecting a visit expecting
the doorbell to ring.

Those sleepy dark lovely eyes . . .

But no love-talk—
I can't take it.
As for love, I just
want to make it.

GEOFFREY BROCK

Prima quando partivi dimenticavi sempre
il tuo profumo, il fazzoletto più bello,
i pantaloni nuovi, i regali per gli amici,
i guanti, gli stivali e l'ombrello.
Questa volta hai lasciato
un paio di mutande
giallo portorico.

Before when you left you would always forget
your perfume, your best handkerchief,
your new pants, your gifts for friends,
your gloves, your boots and your umbrella.
This time you left
a pair of Puerto Rico yellow
underpants.

JUDITH BAUMEL

Seguita la vita come prima
con gente in piedi, seduta,
e che cammina.

Life goes on like before—
people standing, sitting,
and walking.

GINI ALHADEFF

Che m'importa del tuo naso gonfio.
Io devo pulire la casa.

What do I care if your nose is all swollen.
I have to clean the house.

GINI ALHADEFF

Ma prima bisogna liberarsi
dall'avarizia esatta che ci produce,
che me produce seduta
nell'angolo di un bar
ad aspettare con passione impiegatizia
il momento preciso nel quale
il focarello azzurro degli occhi
opposti degli occhi acclimatati
al rischio, calcolata la traiettoria,
pretenderà un rossore
dal mio viso. E un rossore otterrà.

But first we must free ourselves
from the strict stinginess that produces us,
that produces me on this chair
in the corner of a café
awaiting with the ardor of a clerk
the very moment in which
the small blue flames of the eyes
across from me, eyes familiar
with risk, will, having taken aim,
lay claim to a blush
from my face. Which blush they will obtain.

GEOFFREY BROCK

I marocchini con i tappeti
sembrano santi e invece
sono mercanti.

The Moroccans with the carpets
seem like saints
but they're salesmen.

KENNETH KOCH

from

il cielo 1981

A OKAPI BANDIERINA

*Tu non sei stata mai sentimentale
e io per amore voglio assomigliarti.*

from

the sky <small>1981</small>

TO OKAPI BANDIERINA

You were never sentimental and
out of love I'd like to be like you.

Ah sì, per tua disgrazia,
invece di partire
sono rimasta a letto.

Io sola padrona della casa
ho chiuso la porta
ho tirato le tende.
E fuori i quattro canarini
ingabbiati sembravano quattro foreste
e le quattromila voci dei risvegli
confuse dal ritorno della luce.
Ma al di là della porta
nei corridoi bui, nelle stanze
quasi vuote che catturano
i suoni più lontani
i passi miserabili di languidi ritorni
a casa, si accendevano nascite
e pericoli, si consumavano
morti losche e indifferenti.

E cosa credi che io non t'abbia visto
morire dietro un angolo
con il bicchiere che ti cadeva dalle mani
il collo rosso e gonfio
vergognandoti un poco
per essere stata sorpresa

Ah yes, to your misfortune,
instead of leaving
I stayed in bed.

I, sole mistress of the house,
closed the door,
drew the blinds.
And outside, the four caged
canaries sounded like four forests
and four thousand voices reawakening
confused by the return of light.
But beyond the door
in the dark halls, in the nearly
empty rooms that capture
the furthest sounds,
the pitiful steps of languid homecomings,
births and hazards were kindled,
indifferent and shady deaths
were consumed.

And what do you think, that I couldn't see you
die around a corner
with the glass falling from your hands
your neck red and swollen
a little ashamed
to have been surprised

ancora una volta
dopo tanto tempo
nella stessa posizione nella stessa condizione
pallida tremante piena di scuse?

Ma se poi penso veramente alla tua morte
in quale letto d'ospedale o casa o albergo,
in quale strada, magari in aria
o in una galleria; ai tuoi occhi che cedono
sotto l'invasione, all'estrema terribile bugia
con la quale vorrai respingere l'attacco
o l'infiltrazione, al tuo sangue pulsare indeciso
e forsennato nell'ultima immensa visione
di un insetto di passaggio, di una piega di lenzuolo,
di un sasso o di una ruota
che ti sopravviveranno,
allora come faccio a lasciarti andar via?

yet another time
after so much time
in the same position, the same condition,
pale, trembling, filled with excuses?

But then if I really think about your death
in whatever house, hotel or hospital bed,
in whatever street, perhaps in air
or in a tunnel; about your eyes that surrender
to the invasion; about the ultimate terrible lie
with which you will want to repulse the attack
on the infiltration; about your blood pulsing hesitant
and frantic in the final immense vision
of a passing insect, of a fold in the sheet,
of a stone or a wheel
that will survive you
well then, how can I let you go away?

JUDITH BAUMEL

Quando si è colti all'improvviso da salute
lo sguardo non inciampa, non resta appiccicato,
ma lievemente si incanta sulle cose ferme
e sul fermento e le immagini sono risucchiate
e scivolano dentro
come nel gatto che socchiudendo gli occhi mi saluta.

I rumori si sciolgono: i gridi e le sirene
semplicemente sono. La tessitura sgranata
degli odori riporta ogni lontananza
e la memoria, inventando i suoni, fa cantare
alla voce una canzone che avanza
fra il traffico e le spinte.

E certo noi eravamo nati
per questa consonanza.
Ma vivendo in città c'è sempre
qua e là una qualche improvvisa puzza
di fritto che ti rimanda a casa.

When one finds one's self unexpectedly selected by health,
one's gaze does not trip, won't inadvertently stick,
but faintly wondrously grows attached
to hard matter, still matter, that leavening,
where images are swallowed up, where they slip down into one, easy,
as into this cat which clenches its eyes just now to greet me.

The sounds dissolve: the cries the sirens:
they shall simply *be*. The raveling fabrics of odors
carry in themselves to us
all depths of field, disappearance, memory,
making up sound, making voice sing
song that forces itself through morning traffic
through rudeness crowd.

Yes we were born
for this terrible assonance.
But the city gives you, always, unexpectedly,
here and there, out of nowhere, and immediately, its stench,
burnt oil, fried food, to send you home.

JORIE GRAHAM

Non giochi più, mangi soltanto,
ma il tuo collo rimane piccolo.
E hai tante pulci!

You no longer play, you only eat,
Yet your neck is so thin.
And you are covered with fleas!

J. D. MCCLATCHY

Mangiava una mela Macintosh
e mi mostrava labbra spiegazzate.
E alla fine non sapeva cosa fare
nemmeno riusciva a buttare
quel piccolo maciullamento che sempre più
gli si ingialliva in mano.

È di giorno che bisogna ubriacarsi
quando il corpo ancora aspetta sorprese
dalla luce e dal movimento,
quando ancora possiede energie
per inventare un disastro.

Eating a Macintosh apple
she showed me her crumpled lips.
And afterwards she didn't know what to do
she couldn't even discard
that small mangled thing that more and more
turned yellow in her hand.

And daylight's the time to get drunk
when the body still waits for surprises
from light and from rhythm,
when it still has the energy
to invent a disaster.

DAVID SHAPIRO WITH

GINI ALHADEFF

Mi ero tagliata i capelli, scurite le sopracciglia,
aggiustata la piega destra della bocca, assottigliato
il corpo, alzata la statura. Avevo anche regalato
alle spalle un ammiccamento trionfante. Ecco ragazza
ragazzo
di nuovo, per le strade, il passo del lavoratore,
niente abbellimenti superflui. Ma non avevo dimenticato
il languore della sedia, la nuvola della vista.
E spargevo carezze, senza accorgermene. Il mio corpo
segreto intoccabile. Nelle reni
si condensava l'attesa senza soddisfazione; nei giardini
le passeggiate, la ripetizione dei consigli,
il cielo qualche volta azzurro
e qualche volta no.

I had cut my hair, darkened my eyebrows,
adjusted the right fold of my mouth, thinned
my body, raised my height. I had even lent
the shoulders a triumphant bent. A girl
                              boy
again, on the streets, a workman's gait,
no superfluous embellishments. But I hadn't forgotten
the languor of the chair, a clouded vision.
And I distributed caresses, not knowing I did. My secret
body untouchable. In the lower back
expectation condensed without satisfaction; in the gardens
long walks, advice repeated,
the sky sometimes blue
sometimes not.

GINI ALHADEFF

Adesso che il tempo sembra tutto mio
e nessuno mi chiama per il pranzo e per la cena,
adesso che posso rimanere a guardare
come si scioglie una nuvola e come si scolora,
come cammina un gatto per il tetto
nel lusso immenso di una esplorazione, adesso
che ogni giorno mi aspetta
la sconfinata lunghezza di una notte
dove non c'è richiamo e non c'è più ragione
di spogliarsi in fretta per riposare dentro
l'accecante dolcezza di un corpo che mi aspetta,
adesso che il mattino non ha mai principio
e silenzioso mi lascia ai miei progetti
a tutte le cadenze della voce, adesso
vorrei improvvisamente la prigione.

Now that time seems all mine
and no one calls me for lunch or dinner,
now that I can stay to watch
how a cloud loosens and loses its color,
how a cat walks on the roof
in the immense luxury of a prowl, now
that what waits for me every day
is the unlimited length of a night
where there is no call and no longer a reason
to undress in a hurry to rest inside
the blinding sweetness of a body that waits for me,
now that the morning never has a beginning
and silently leaves me to my plans,
to all the cadences of voice, now
suddenly I would like prison.

JUDITH BAUMEL

Così arrivi, come sempre,
a spargere il sospetto del paradiso,
e prima ancora di aprire la finestra
ti riconosco dalla luce più lenta
dai pulviscoli sospesi e senza direzione
dalla replica ossessiva degli uccelli,
e se non fossero gli uccelli sarebbe un'altra cosa,
per ogni posto hai le tue specialità;
e quando entri e ti lascio i miei sensi
riabito cose sconosciute e ho nostalgia
di cose mai avvenute. E attraverso i tuoi labirinti
sospingi addosso a me i continenti e le stagioni
e io divento la parete degli urti e dei rimbalzi
l'appoggio dove cominciano le fughe
fino al risucchio silenzioso dell'estate.

You arrive like this, as always,
to spread the suspicion of paradise,
and before I open the window
I know you from the gentler light,
from the dust that hangs in the air,
from the birds' obsessive performance,
and if it weren't the birds it would be something else,
for you have your specialties for every place;
and when you come in and I surrender my senses
I'm living in unfamiliar houses again and feeling nostalgia
for things that never occurred. And across your labyrinths
you hang the continents and seasons on my back
and I become the wall of shouts and reflections
the platform flights take off from
till the silent eddies of summer.

JONATHAN GALASSI

Che la morte mi avvenga dentro un desiderio
oltrepassando un uscio, ché altrimenti
non potrei sopportare che piano piano
mi si svanisca dagli occhi
o dalla memoria il lenzuolo celeste,
la coperta bianca, la luce bellissima
che schiariva la stanza.

Non come il gatto bianco e nero
che vedo morire lentamente imprigionato
dentro i suoi viaggi dove si ferma,
sbalordito di sé, per una riconquista
delle direzioni verso una certa sedia
un certo termosifone e guardando un po' a destra
e un po' a sinistra prosegue verso un muro
che non era nelle sue intenzioni.
Ma ancora gli rimane, toccando appena
la sua testa o dicendo il suo nome,
l'esplosione famosa delle fusa.

A mia nonna era rimasta una qualità
nervosa, un fastidio per gli altri,
il ricordo sicuro delle sue antipatie.

Let death come to me wrapped in a wish
past a door, or
I couldn't bear it if gently gently
from my eyes
or from my memory the pale blue sheet
the white blanket, the dazzling light
that lit up the room were to withdraw.

Unlike the black and white cat
I see slowly dying trapped
in his travels when he stops,
surprising himself, to regain
his bearings towards a certain chair
a certain radiator and looking to the right a little
and to the left proceeds towards a wall
which was not part of his plan.
But still in his powers, if you touch
his head or say his name,
is the famous explosion of purrs.

All my grandmother had left was a nervous
quality, a distaste for others,
the certain memory of her dislikes.

GINI ALHADEFF

È inutile fare sforzi
diventare più adulti, più maturi
interessarsi alle tante sorti
del mondo nei giornali
e intanto guardare con sensi approssimati
scomparse e ricomparse
dentro e fuori e i minuscoli regali
della memoria inacidita
nelle scatole e nelle scatolette.

There's no point in trying
to become more adult, more mature,
take an interest in the many fates
of the world in the papers
while gazing with sketchy senses
at disappearances and reappearances
ins and outs and the minuscule gifts
of memory soured
in boxes and smaller boxes.

GINI ALHADEFF

Come se fosse una spanatura
la luce troppo bianca
mi avvolgeva capitata così all'improvviso
fuori stagione e io impreparata
non volevo pensarci, quasi non guardavo
i campi spelacchiati (ma perché se era
primavera?) colorati di albetta
e mi chiudevo nella simmetria
delle stanze. Ma lì c'era mio padre,
la testa fuori dal cuscino, messo per storto,
non ben sistemato, le pantofole infilate,
coperto a metà così da non sembrare
proprio stabilmente a letto
ma come di passaggio—mi riposo
un momento e ricomincio—
pronto a trascinarsi a la sala comandi,
la cucina, e lì davanti al tavolo impazzare
nella grande sistemazione di piatti
e bottigliette e bruciare nei centimetri quadrati
i movimenti adorati della vita.

As though out of register
the too white light
enveloped me coming all at once
out of season and I was unprepared
I didn't want to think about it, almost didn't look
at the balding fields (but why
if it was springtime?) tinted by new dawn
and I locked myself into the symmetry
of the rooms. But there was my father,
his head off the pillow, laid out crooked,
not properly arranged, with slippers on his feet,
and only half covered so as not to seem
really put to bed
but as if in transit—I rest
a moment and start again—
ready to drag himself to the control room,
the kitchen, and go wild before the table
in a grand shuffling of dishes
and little bottles to burn in square centimeters
the sweet movements of life.

GINI ALHADEFF

Dopo anni tormenti e pentimenti
quello che scopro e quello che mi resta
è una banalità fresca e indigesta.

After years of torment years of regret
what I discover and what I have left
is a banality fresh and hard to digest.

GINI ALHADEFF

Due ore fa mi sono innamorata.
Tremo d'amore e seguito a tremare,
ma non so bene a chi mi devo dichiarare.

Two hours ago I fell in love
and trembled, and tremble still,
and haven't a clue whom I should tell.

MARK STRAND

from

l'io singolare proprio mio 1992

from
the all mine singular i 1992

Dentro il tuo mare viaggiava la mia nave
dentro quel mare mi sono immersa e nacqui.
Mi colpisce la novità della stagione
e il corpo che si accorge di aver freddo.

Di figura in figura trasmigrava amore,
ora si posa e svela la sua forma.
La riconosco in quel veloce crespo
sulla fronte, piccole onde simili
e contrarie—correva in superficie
uno stupore, un cedimento
nella compattezza, e si incrinava
mutando in tenerezza.

Onto your sea my ship set sail,
into that sea I sank and was born.
I am struck by how strange a season it is
and by how my body feels the cold.

From figure to figure love migrated,
now it stops and shows itself.
I recognize it in that crimpled current
on your forehead, small waves alike
and contrary—and on the surface a kind of awe
moved, surging through
whatever seemed rigid, and gave way,
was transformed into tenderness.

J. D. MCCLATCHY

Giunta a quel punto dove la memoria
per troppa luce quasi si scolora,
raccoglievo in preghiera le tue forme.
Il peso immenso del tuo corpo assente
la notte mi copriva di sudore
e prolungavo ferma il mio risveglio
per accaldarmi dentro il tuo mantello.
Poi m'abbigliavo tutta in quella stoffa
che si mischiava stretta al mio respiro
e attraversavo le conversazioni
attenta a non sgualcire il mio vestito.
Qualche volta però per distrazione
cedendo alle domande dei miei ospiti
mi si impigliava un lembo nella noia
e scivolava via con qualche strappo.
Per restaurare la trama in perfezione
poco sicura delle mie sole mani
ricorrevo al valore del telefono.

Having reached the point where memory
by way of too much light almost loses color
I gathered up your forms in prayer.
The immense weight of your absent body
bathed me in sweat at night
and when I awoke unmoving I prolonged my waking
to warm myself inside your cloak.
Then I dressed up in that cloth
and it was all wrapped up with my breath
and I strode across conversations
trying not to wrinkle my dress.
But sometimes by sheer distraction
giving in to the questions of my guests
a corner got caught by boredom
and slipped away torn here and there.
To restore the weave to perfection
uncertain of my hands alone
I resorted to the virtues of the telephone.

GINI ALHADEFF

Se ora tu bussassi alla mia porta
e ti togliessi gli occhiali
e io togliessi i miei che sono uguali
e poi tu entrassi dentro la mia bocca
senza temere baci disuguali
e mi dicessi: "Amore mio,
ma che è successo?", sarebbe un pezzo
di teatro di successo.

If you knocked now on my door
and if you took off your glasses
and I took off mine which are like yours
and then if you entered my mouth
unafraid of kisses that are not like yours
and said to me: "My love,
is everything alright?"—that would be quite
a piece of theater.

GEOFFREY BROCK

La giornata atlantica

Quando col mio giudizio mi dispongo
alla tiepida pace di ogni giorno,
ai pomeriggi docili, al sonno largo
e naturale, non più nemica al clima
che anzi fermo e uguale mi carezza
—si schiude il grumo delle voci e mi fa entrare
e mi corteggiano gli odori delle strade
e mi concedo agli angoli alle piazze
ai visi di vecchi e di ragazze, e innamorata
casta trovo ogni scusa per poter restare—
improvvisa ritorna la giornata atlantica.

La luce alta, i suoni alti della luce
e si apre la distanza. Basta quel luccichío
di latte alle persiane, quelle fessure d'ombra
dense e profonde, l'abbaglio di frescura,
lo sventolío dei rami dai balconi,
ecco l'estate e il cielo si fa mare.
La città si solleva e veleggiando oscilla
mossa dalle brezze. Chiamati dalle altezze
senza ancoraggio o pesi i miei sensi
non più raccolti ma vagabondi sciolti
soli e assoluti si perdono nell'aria
e a casa mandano notizie di terrore.
Notizie: mentre in casa ogni oggetto

The Atlantic Day

When I use my judgment to open up
to the mild peace of everyday,
to docile afternoons, to broad and natural sleep,
no longer unhappy with the climate
that caresses me, regular, changeless even
—the clot of voices unknots and calls to me
and the smells of the streets seduce me
and I give myself to the corners the piazzas
the faces of old men and girls, and chastely
in love I find every excuse for staying—
suddenly the Atlantic day returns.

The high light, the high sounds of the light,
and distance opens. That milky twinkling
on the shutters is all it takes, those dense, deep
cracks in shadows, the glare of freshness,
the waving branches from the balconies,
and look: it's summer, and the sky is sea.
The city lifts and quivers, sailing,
moved by the breezes. Called from the heights
unanchored, weightless, my senses
no longer gathered but wandering freed
alone and absolute get lost in the air
and send home news of terror.
News: while at home each object

ritrova il suo cassetto il suo scaffale
io divento a me stessa marginale.
La mia materia evapora.

L'isola scura e densa mi riappare.
Quella sostanza spessa, promessa di rimedio,
fammi entrare. Riportami al mio limite
circondami, con le carezze segna i miei contorni,
col peso del tuo corpo dammi corpo.
Ma è il rimedio che produce il male.

finds its drawer, its shelf,
I become marginal to myself.
My matter evaporates.

The dark, dense island reappears.
Thick substance, promise of cure,
let me enter. Bring me back to my boundaries,
embrace me, mark my contours with your caresses,
embody me with the weight of your body.
But it's the remedy that makes the illness.

JONATHAN GALASSI

Mammina mia, dammi la virtù,
slacciami! Si avvicina allegria,
potevo immaginarlo?

Dove mi piacerebbe stare adesso?
Naturalmente innaturale
sempre con te che pure resti uguale.

Mi fermo nei millimetri
del particolare: la parte interna
del labbro inferiore, cisterna

dove cado imbambolata—nòcciolo
di nespola, per arrivare
a quella levigatezza bagnata

tolgo la buccia mangio la nespola.
Dove mi piacerebbe stare adesso
con il sole mezzo addormentato

il rumore allontanato?
Ma qui, senz'altro. Avevo
la risposta e l'ho detta.

Spirituale spirito della bicicletta,
fossi un ragazzo io e una ragazza
tu, fosse il contrario anche,

O lord, lend me virtue,
undo my laces! Cheer draws near,
how could I have imagined it?

Where would I like to be now?
Naturally unnatural
always with you who are always the same.

I linger in millimeters
of a detail: inner part
of the lower lip, cistern

into which I fall dazedly—kernel
of a medlar, to reach
a wet smoothness

I peel off the skin eat the medlar.
Where would I like to be now
with the sun half-asleep

and noise at a distance?
Well, here, no doubt. I had
the answer and I said it.

O spiritual spirit of the bicycle,
if I were a boy and you
a girl, or the other way around,

ti potrei baciare, mi potrei accostare,
potrei succhiare quel nòcciolo di nespola.

La frutta appena comprata
io l'assaggio sempre per strada.

I could kiss you, I could get close,
I could suck the kernel of that medlar.

When I buy fruit I have to taste it
right away out on the street.

GINI ALHADEFF

Il corpo era lenzuolo e si stendeva
per accogliere il mattino tiepido e nuovo
e di nuovo nella luce mi appariva
l'avventura dei visi. Camminando
lasciavo la mia strada
per inseguire spalle curve e spalle altere.
Quanti amori! Poi mi fermavo
a cercare la virtù dei miei pensieri.

The body was a sheet it laid itself out
to receive the morning damp new
and once again in the light it would appear to me
the face the adventure. So walking
I abandoned my journey
to follow those shoulders, proud shoulders, mutable shoulders.
Oh how many loves! Until I would stop and think
and search for the virtue
at the core of my thought.

JORIE GRAHAM

È predisposto per i miei risvegli
un rigido paesaggio
dove non trovo immagini o pensieri
ma lugubri e modesti ragionieri.
Ai bordi del mio sonno a sentinella
sempre a quell'ora vengono a cercarmi
decidono che è l'ora della sveglia.
Contano gli anni subito e i terrori
le perdite i guadagni: in mano loro
il tempo è una fettuccia consumata
la vita sembra ormai persa per strada.

In pieno giorno però io li confondo
non mi metto a competere con loro
faccio finta di niente e l'imbavaglio
poi li copro di stracci e li strapazzo
mi mostro sempre più smodata e futile.
Moriranno anche loro, sì, che muoiano,
canaglie stupide ignoranti, che ne sanno?
Non sanno mica che sono io lo sbaglio.

Again it has prepared itself for my awakening
the intransigent horizon its landscape its hills
empty of images empty of thought
except for the unending gloom into which
the accountants put forth their modest spreadsheets.
And at the edge of my sleep always the sentinels.
Always at that hour coming to find me.
They set the alarm they set the awakening.
And yes immediately they add up the years, the terrors, the losses,
    the gains,
in their hands time the ribbon consumes itself
subtracting adding how is it that life
got lost or left behind, and where down that road?

In broad daylight on the other hand I shall mistake them,
I shall not compete with them,
I shall act like it's nothing, absolutely nothing, and gag them
and cover them with rags and exhaust them
showing myself to be ever more uncouth and vain.
They too shall die. Yes. Let them die.
Scoundrels, rogues—what do they know?
How would they ever know I am the error?

JORIE GRAHAM

Ma davvero per uscire di prigione
bisogna conoscere il legno della porta,
la lega delle sbarre, stabilire l'esatta
gradazione del colore? A diventare
così grandi esperti, si corre il rischio
che poi ci si affezioni. Se vuoi uscire
davvero di prigione, esci subito,
magari con la voce, diventa una canzone.

To get out of prison do you really need
to know what wood the door is made of,
the alloy of the bars, the precise hue
of the walls? Becoming so expert, you might
grow too fond of the place. If you really do
want out, don't wait so long, leave now,
maybe use your voice, become a song.

GEOFFREY BROCK

Non affidarti alla mia immaginazione
non ti fidare, io non ti conservo,
non ti metto da parte per l'inverno,
io ti apro e ti mangio in un boccone.

Don't count on my imagination, no,
don't count on that, I won't preserve you,
won't put you on the shelf till winter,
I'll open you now and swallow you whole.

GEOFFREY BROCK

Penso che forse a forza di pensarti
potrò dimenticarti, amore mio.

Thinking about you
might let me forget you, my love.

MARK STRAND

Ora nell'umore del vino torno
alla mia vera pulsazione. E salendo le scale
mi appoggio, ferma alle venature del marmo.
Mia prigione, mio trasloco, io cado
nella tua presenza, assenza mia.
Sembra uno spreco questo lusso postumo.
Ma sembra vero. Fammi nuotare.

Now wine in my blood I turn again
to my real thrum, my pulse, and climbing these stairs once more
lean to the wall to steady myself, for there they are again the veins
    their marble,
my prison my transfer station my place to fall
into your presence beloved nothingness
who seem like a waste, you, luscious posthumousness,
yet are so real. Let me swim into you.

JORIE GRAHAM

Solo a sentire un verbo
che mi sembri vero
sento corrermi il sangue
alla salvezza. Come tornare a casa
e ritrovare pietosa freschezza di lenzuola.

Just hearing a verb
that sounds true to me
I feel my blood spurting
towards salvation. Like coming home
and finding the merciful fresh sheet.

DAVID SHAPIRO WITH

GINI ALHADEFF

Tra un po' tutti all'inferno.
Però per il momento
è finita l'estate.
Avanti, su, ai divani!
Ai divani! Ai divani!

We're all going to hell in a while.
But meanwhile
summer's over.
So come on now, to the couch!
The couch! The couch!

GINI ALHADEFF

Era questa la madre che volevo,
scura e malinconica
lontana dal mondo
ansiosa.
Parla poco e si mangia le parole.
Cade qualche volta e si rialza in fretta.
Era questa la madre che volevo,
scura dolorosa
zoppa
e ho lottato contro le sorelle
ho distrutto i fratelli
perché era questa la madre che volevo,
volenterosa ampia chiusa prigioniera.
Non volevo altra madre che questa,
capelli mal cresciuti che non trovano
forma né pace, la copia trasandata
di se stessa, sfatta di dolcezza,
l'unico lusso era la sua fuga
davanti allo specchio
mentre si vestiva.

Davanti allo specchio mentre si vestiva
lo sguardo le si divaricava
perduto in una immagine futura,
la prima ladra in lei riconoscevo

This was the mother I wanted
dark and melancholic
far from the world
anxious.
She hardly speaks and chews her words.
She falls down sometimes and gets up quickly.
This was the mother I wanted
dark grieving
lame
and I struggled against the sisters
demolished the brothers
because this was the mother I wanted
willing ample closed imprisoned.
I wanted no other mother,
badly grown hair that finds
neither form nor peace, the shabby copy
of herself, undone by sweetness,
the only luxury was her escape
before the mirror
as she dressed.

Before the mirror as she dressed
her glance would stray
to a future image,
I saw in her the first thief

che mi rubava l'immagine sicura
e la portava fuori e regalava
quello che solo mio essere doveva.

who stole from me the safe image,
took it outside and dispensed
what should have been mine alone.

GINI ALHADEFF

Niente nella testa. Foresta chiusa inabitata.
Le erbe i fiori i pollini le foglie
volano fuori dalla mia finestra.
Dura ancora natura e è sicura,
quest'anno ha colori cattivissimi.

Vacant head. Uninhabited shut woods.
The grass the flowers the pollen the leaves
flying out now through my window.
For now it endures, nature, for now still safe.
This year growing colors crueler than ever.

JORIE GRAHAM

Ah smetti sedia di esser così sedia!
E voi, libri, non siate così libri!
Come le metti stanno, le giacche abbandonate.
Troppa materia, troppa identità.
Tutti padroni della propria forma.
Sono. Sono quel che sono. Solitari.
E io li vedo a uno a uno separati
e ferma anch'io faccio da piazzetta
a questi oggetti fermi, soli, raggelati.
Ci vuole molta ariosa tenerezza,
una fretta pietosa che muova e che confonda
queste forme padrone sempre uguali, perché
non è vero che si torna, non si ritorna
al ventre, si parte solamente,
si diventa singolari.

Chair, stop being such a chair!
And books, don't you be books like that!
They're there the way you left them, jackets sloughed.
Too much matter, too much identity.
Each one the master of its form.
They are. They are what they are. By themselves.
And I see them separate one by one
and I'm planted too like a little square
for these objects—solid, single, frozen.
It will take a lot of airy tenderness,
a sympathetic flurry to move and rearrange
these master-forms that never change, because
it's not true we come back, we don't go back
to the womb, we only leave,
we become singular.

JONATHAN GALASSI

Qualcosa che all'oggetto non s'apprende,
un secchio vuoto che non mi raccoglie.
Tenevo i mesi silenziosi in una trama
che doveva risplendere di voce.
Provavo a dire e mi si sfilacciava.
Non è né rete né mantello, è solo schermo,
io non catturo niente e non mi copre
ma separa un silenzio dal silenzio.
Quell'altro suono labirintico e interiore
esercitato in solitudine per strada
e nei risvegli, non risultava,
non mi si mostrava.

Something that the object never can take in,
an empty bucket that won't carry me.
I held the silent months in a wide weave
which was supposed to flash forth in full voice.
I tried to speak and it unraveled on my tongue.
It's neither net nor coat, it's only a screen;
I capture nothing and it won't cover me
but separates one silence from the silence.
That other labyrinthine and interior sound
practiced alone as I walk along the street
or waking up, did not emerge,
held off from me.

ROSANNA WARREN

Stai ferma a capotavola
grassa di vino,
inorgoglita dalle mie lagrime
fai la lezione.
Ma sono io che piango
e non mi muovo,
tu alzati, fa qualcosa,
togli i piatti!

You sit at the head of the table
heady with wine,
and hold forth,
made proud by my tears.
But I'm the one who's crying
and I won't move.
So you get up, be useful,
pick up the plates!

MARK STRAND WITH

GINI ALHADEFF

Ormai è sicuro, il mondo non esiste
la sua materia labile che si trasforma
in gioia o dannazione. Quella parete
quella parete, quella strada, quel muro,
quell'occasione infetta che è nella mia testa.
I pensierini. Il tempo.
Mi scivola via l'anima
e io non la trattengo.

Now it's sure, the world doesn't exist
its labile matter that transforms into
joy or damnation. That wall,
that wall, that street, that building side,
the infected happening in my head.
Those little thoughts. And time.
The spirit slips away
and I don't hold it.

JONATHAN GALASSI

Prima era facile il pensiero lieve
bocciolo di garofano
che ambiva solo a aprirsi vanitoso,
che se restava chiuso poi appassiva.
Ora questo nuovo pensiero duro
che non s'apre e non decade,
questo cespo spinoso sempreverde
che il gelo non secca, che il sole
non accende, che cresce basso basso
attorto su se stesso sempre uguale
e complicandosi non sale, costretto,
soltanto perché è nato, a perdurare.

At first the little thought was easy
a carnation bud
that only wanted to open narcissistically,
for if it stayed shut it would wilt.
Now this hard new thought
that will not open or decay,
this spiny bush of evergreen
which cold won't burn, which sun cannot ignite,
which hugs the ground
bent on itself unchanging
and contortedly won't rise,
compelled, by being born, to last.

JONATHAN GALASSI

Natale. La festa della luce.
Si ricomincia insomma.
Una paura selvatica.
Così si fa casetta
e ci si attruppa caldi
e gonfi, stremati.

Ma anche, chiamati
in segreto dall'inizio,
si vuole uscire
per provare la forza
delle gambe, darsi alla macchia
al freddo—Vediamo
quanto duro coi cinghiali.

Christmas. Festival of light.
In other words: you must begin again.
Oh savage fear.
So build the little house again
and gather yourself up into it
hot-blooded swollen torn.

And even if the beginning
calls to you ferociously, furtively,
you will not listen, you'll want to flee, to
test the strength of
limbs, to give yourself
to the woods, to the cold. Let's see
how long I'll last—
you think to yourself—
among the boars.

JORIE GRAHAM

"Vado, ma dove? oh dei!"
Sempre al bar, al ristorante, nei musei
a ciondolare anoressica o bulimica
sempre tra le due madri
quella che mi ama falsamente
e mi vorrebbe privare di ogni cibo
e l'altra che mi ama falsamente
e mi vorrebbe uccidere di cibo,
e io costretta a uno dei due eccessi
o l'astinenza o l'incontinenza
e intanto guardo il bel viso di un ragazzo
sempre lontano dai miei veri amori
spinta al turismo da cerberi
infelici viaggiatori.

"I'm going, but where? Oh gods!"
Always to cafés, restaurants, museums,
swaying anorexic or bulimic
between two mothers as always
this one who loves me falsely
and would deny me all food
that one who loves me falsely
and would kill me with food,
and me forced to choose one or the other
starve or binge and meanwhile
I'm staring at a boy's beautiful face
a far cry from my true loves,
hounded into tourism by those
wretched roving watchdogs.

GEOFFREY BROCK

Io scientificamente mi domando
come è stato creato il mio cervello,
cosa ci faccio io con questo sbaglio.
Fingo di avere anima e pensieri
per circolare meglio in mezzo agli altri,
qualche volta mi sembra anche di amare
facce e parole di persone, rare;
esser toccata vorrei poter toccare,
ma scopro sempre che ogni mia emozione
dipende da un vicino temporale.

Scientifically I wonder
how it was my brain was made,
what I'm doing here with this blunder.
I pretend to have a soul and thoughts
so as to better be around others
sometimes I even think I'm touched
by faces and words of people—not much;
being touched I'd like to touch,
but then discover that every one of my emotions
is due to some approaching thunder.

GINI ALHADEFF

Non più narcisa, la vanità perduta,
cosa mi resta? Un ibrido di attese
e mal di testa. Il pensiero mi manca
il passo arranca, questo nuovo peccato,
la santità.

A narcissist no more, vanity gone,
what's left? A mix of waiting
and headaches. Thoughts fail me,
I drag my feet, my latest sin
sanctity.

MARK STRAND WITH

GINI ALHADEFF

from
sempre aperto teatro 1999

from
the forever
open theater 1999

O amori—veri o falsi
siate amori, muovetevi felici
nel vuoto che vi offro.

O loves—true or false
be loves, move happily
in the void I offer you.

Balia mite e pensosa
sono di questo amore
fiacco: lo curo lo trastullo
e non mi arrabbio, i suoi pochi
bisogni io soddisfo, preparo
buone cene e vado a letto.
Poi d'improvviso dico, ma solo
tra me e me: "E se l'ammazzo?"

I am the mild and obedient nurse
to this worn-out love.
I care for it, cradle it,
hold my temper;
I satisfy its few needs,
make good dinners, go to bed;
then all of a sudden
I say to myself: "What if I killed her?"

MARK STRAND WITH

GINI ALHADEFF

Quando, per i pregi del vino,
io mi dimentico della memoria
solida e lievemente possibile
mi appare quel mio piacere
per il profumo assorbito di nascosto
nel cesso di un amico che usa
quel profumo, e sto per parcheggiare,
e mi dico: "Avanti, muoviti, va' per la città,
non troverai niente, però forse
vedrai una luce accesa. Sei innamorata,
e fa' l'innamorata! Gli innamorati
non vanno forse come pazzi su e giù
per una strada?" E poi mi fermo,
perché ho trovato facile il parcheggio,
allora ferma, morbidamente
ferma, ti assumo mia, docile
ritardo del mio amore.

When, thanks to the virtues of wine,
I let go of solid memory and a certain pleasure
seems almost real to me
having secretly picked up a scent
in the john of a friend who uses that scent
and I'm about to park,
and I say to myself: "Go on, move, drive around the city,
you won't find anything, but maybe
you'll see a light on. You're in love, aren't you?
So act like someone in love! Don't people in love
drive up and down streets like crazy?"
But then, because I found easy parking,
I stop, and while I'm stopped, comfortably stopped,
I imagine you, in the helpless delay of my love, as mine.

MARK STRAND WITH

GINI ALHADEFF

Ah sì, si è fidanzata?
Allora è fidanzata.
Davvero è fidanzata?
Dunque si è fidanzata.
Ma è proprio fidanzata?
Beh, insomma è fidanzata.
Dici che è fidanzata?
Va bene, è fidanzata.

Oh really, she's with somebody?
So she's with somebody.
Is she really with somebody?
I guess she's with somebody.
So she is actually with somebody?
Well then, she is, she's with somebody.
So you're saying she's with somebody?
Okay, then, she's with somebody.

MARK STRAND WITH

GINI ALHADEFF

Ma quei ragazzi con le gambe storte
che avanzano con passi truci e assorti,
sorelle permalose, timide spose,
perché non li vedevo, ora dov'erano?

Uno alla volta davanti mi sfilavano
entrando al cinema, io ferma sulla porta
sfacciatamente intenta li osservavo
cercando quello che lei avrebbe amato,
pronta ad amarlo anch'io se lo trovavo.
Però nessuno mi sembrava bello,
proprio nessuno, per quanto mi sforzassi
erano goffi, grigi, rozzi, grassi.
Sicura che avrei subito imparato
mi trasferivo in lei e la imitavo,
ma troppa mira fa lo sguardo angusto,
amor traslato non coglie mai nel giusto.

But those kids with twisted legs
moving so menacing and self-absorbed,
haughty sisters, timid wives,
why did I not see them, where were they now?

One by one they passed in front of me
entering the theater; I at the door
stood staring openly
searching for what she would have loved,
ready to love it too if I could find it.
But none of them was beautiful to me,
not one, and though I tried to force myself
they were awkward, gray, crude, fat.
Convinced I would have quickly learned
I made myself be her and acted like her.
But too much searching makes one's look too tight;
love that's translated never turns out right.

JONATHAN GALASSI

Nello schiumoso caldo quasi indiano
di un luglio cittadino esagerato
i residui abitanti con cautela
siedono lungamente nei caffè
cercando illusi l'aria che non c'è.
In casa chiusa, priva di faccende
io mi affaccendo intorno alla tua faccia
che entra indifferente nella mischia
dei miei pensieri e ne esce sempre intatta,
come fosse un mammozzolo di gomma
che anche a contorcerlo e a schiacciarlo
sempre ritrova la sua prima forma,
l'inerte galleggiante della mente
che più lo immergi e più violento emerge.

In the seething almost Indian heat
of an exaggerated July in the city
the remaining inhabitants cautiously
sit at length in the cafés
looking for air that is not there.
In my closed house, with nothing to do,
I busy myself with your face
which coolly enters the war
of my thoughts and leaves intact,
as though it were a rubber blob
that even if it's pushed or squeezed
always goes back to its original shape,
the inert buoy of the mind
which the more you push it down
the more it pops back up.

MARK STRAND WITH

GINI ALHADEFF

L'amore non è certo un sentimento
ma è quell'ossessivo ragionare
sul mistero del nostro apprendimento.
Apprendo la tua faccia e la mantengo
ma poi la perdo in un istante e la riprendo,
aggiungo e tolgo, mi accorgo
di ogni cambiamento, funambolo pensiero
sempre sul punto di cadere
—amore non sostiene.

No, love surely isn't a feeling,
it's an obsessive line of thought
about the mystery of how we learn.
I take in your face and hold it fast
but then I lose it quick as a wink, and take it back,
I add and subtract, I register
each shade of change: a tightrope-walking thought
always about to fall—
love doesn't hold.

ROSANNA WARREN

Ferma d'improvviso senza meta
sull'ultimo gradino di una scala
che in nessun posto più mi conduceva
stringendo con la mano la ringhiera
sollevai gli occhi. Ah che cosa era
quell'ovale fervore della porta
che stava chiusa e assorta nel suo stato?
Io come forestiera la guardavo
lo sguardo ormai lasciato alla preghiera
il resto del mio corpo si scioglieva
salendo come spirito alla bocca.
Per conservare forza al mio pensiero
su quella stessa scala mi sedevo
dicendo con la voce: "E' strano, è strano,
ah io da qui però non me ne vado
senza capire, è strano, è così strano."
Ma più violentemente mi perdevo
in un languore bianco senza storia
memoria precedente a ogni memoria
come fosse una mischia originaria
dove vagassero cellule che ancora
non si erano aggregate nell'umano
presente che noi siamo. E finalmente
priva di pensiero quasi cedevo
del tutto a questa larga nostalgia
che mi portava via con sé lontano

Stopping suddenly, no destination
at the top of stairs
that no longer led me anywhere
I held the banister
and raised my eyes. Ah what was
the oval fervor of that portal,
shut and absorbed in its condition?
Like a foreigner I gaped at it
my look now given to prayer
the rest of my body slack
rising like spirit to my mouth.
To conserve the strength of my idea
I sat down on the stairs
and said aloud: "It's strange, it's strange.
And I'm not leaving here until
I understand. It's strange, so strange."
But I got lost more violently
in a white languor with no history
a memory before all other memory
like an original mélange
in which cells could wander
that still had not agglomerated
into the human present that we are. And finally
empty of thought I nearly gave in
fully to this broad nostalgia
that took me far away with it

togliendomi alla mia cronologia.
Ma la vile indolenza del mio cuore
capace solo di superstizione
subito chiuse quell'empito in un nome
e lo spazioso caldo senza nome
prese la forma e il gelido colore
dell'ultimo recluso suo rifugio.
E mi trovai nel buio dell'amore.

and deprived me of my own chronology.
But my heart's vile laziness
that's only capable of superstition
soon encased that impetus in a name
and the spacious, nameless heat
took the form and cold
of its last shut refuge.
And I found myself in the dark of love.

JONATHAN GALASSI

Come ero lì, e forse c'era un fiume,
e questa luce estiva d'improvviso
smessa, dolcemente scurita da nuvole novelle
delicate. Sì c'era il fiume
e la freschezza grigia. E come
calpestavo il tempo, come non c'era
il tempo, ferma dentro ogni giorno
che assorbivo; e queste superfici di persone,
questi corpi diversi con braccia
facce e gambe che si mostrano,
che per essere lì in quella piazza, così
come attraversano lo spazio aperto al sole
e come poi rientrano nell'ombra,
hanno subito il tempo per esser come sono,
ma se li guardo,
salvi dalla storia in quel momento
quando li accolgo.

How I was there and maybe there was a river
and this summer light unexpectedly ceased
gently darkened by nervous newly arriving delicate
clouds. Yes the river was there
and the gray fresh air. And as I
trampled time, as there was in fact
no time, locked as I was into
each day, soaking it in, and these surfaces of personhood,
these scattered limbs,
arms faces legs,
showing themselves to us,
showing us how it is to be there, in that piazza, how to
cross its space open to sun and then
reenter shade, having undergone time,
to be as they are,
except that if I look at them,
there, in that instant,
they are rescued from history
where I greet them.

JORIE GRAHAM

Che tristezza un'ossatura rumorosa!
Ricordarsi ogni momento dello scheletro
che la carne, finché può, copre pietosa.

The sadness of creaking limbs!
To be reminded again and again
of the skeleton, which the flesh,
as long as it lasts, mercifully covers.

MARK STRAND

Affresco della notte palombara
immersa nel recinto di figure
strette all'attore, custodia di parole,
fame e miniera di nostalgia alle due
del pomeriggio, l'ora di mezzo
priva di preghiere, che non presume
ma si affatica strana dietro l'immensità
del pomeriggio, molto popolata immensità
di guarigione, che si allontana
insieme al tuo silenzio intento e affaccendato
a togliermi dal sole, mio sole virtuoso
per il quale io sono quel che sono
in piena luce, sono nel mondo
assieme agli altri, agli altri quasi uguale.

Fresco of the underwater night
sunk in a knot of figures
surrounding the actor, keeper of words;
hunger and quarry of longing
at two p.m., the middle hour
without prayer that doesn't presume
but labors strangely over the afternoon's
hugeness, crowded hugeness
of healing that drifts off;
and your focused silence bent on
taking my sun, my virtuous sun,
thanks to which I am what I am
in daylight, I am in the world
with others, others almost like me.

JONATHAN GALASSI

Com'era dolce ieri immaginarmi albero!
Mi ero quasi in un punto radicata
e lì crescevo in lentezza sovrana.
Io ricevevo brezza e tramontana,
carezze o scuotimenti, che importava?
Non ero io a me stessa gioia né tormento,
io non potevo togliermi al mio centro,
io senza decisioni o movimento,
se mi muovevo era per il vento.

How sweet it was yesterday imagining I was a tree!
I had almost rooted in one place
and grew in sovereign slowness there.
I took the breeze and the north wind,
caresses, blows—what difference did it make?
I was neither joy nor torment to myself,
I couldn't detach myself from my own center,
no decisions, no movement:
if I moved it was because of the wind.

JONATHAN GALASSI

Ognuno ha il suo mistero,
il mio è il mal di testa,
com'è che mi ridesta sempre l'amore?
Vieni, mio amore, vieni, ho il mal di testa.

Il mal di testa abbatte la memoria,
ma se la testa perde la memoria
c'è il cuore che raccoglie la memoria,
ma il cuore è atemporale senza storia,
così vecchio dolore diventi gioia nuova.

Everyone has a mystery,
mine is headaches,
why do they always reawaken love in me?
Come, my love, come, I have a headache.

Headaches maim memory
if the head loses its memory
there's the heart to hoard memory,
the heart is atemporal without history,
you, my old sorrow, might turn into fresh joy.

GINI ALHADEFF

Ma voi siete cristiani?
Allora siate cristiani.
La sera si potrebbe.
È per questo potere che è la vita,
questo ritardo. Questi mazzi di fiori
non portati, poi in un sol colpo
in morte consegnati. Quanti fiori!
Eppure si potrebbe.

Uscire, varcare, raggiungere.

But you, are you Christians?
So be it, you are Christians.
At night one could be.
So for this might
it is thought to be life,
this lateness, this aftermath . . . These bouquets of flowers
left undelivered, in one fell swoop now
felled, extinguished. So many flowers!
And yet, one could . . .

Exit, cross over, exceed, reach.

JORIE GRAHAM

Io quegli isotopi non li voglio bevere,
la mia tiroide non la voglio perdere.
Per gentilezza si è ammalata, per difendermi
da altri più vili attacchi innaturali
ha chiuso le sue porte e in autarchia
si è troppo follemente sviluppata.
E adesso io modernamente ingrata
dovrei sopprimerla in quanto malattia?
No, i miei amici io non li tradisco
se hanno sbagliato per troppa solerzia.
E fosse pure che così guarisco,
poi che peccato morire perfetta.

I those isotopes don't want to drink
my thyroid I do not want to lose.
Out of kindness it fell ill, to defend me
from other more vicious unnatural attacks
it shut its doors and in autarchy
too madly it developed.
And now modernly ungrateful
I should suppress it as an illness?
No, my friends I do not betray
if they made a mistake out of too much zeal.
Even if that were to make me well,
and besides what a pity to die perfect.

MARK STRAND WITH

GINI AHADEFF

D'improvviso come fosse un raffreddore
torna l'amore. Non è un raffreddore
è un mal di testa che toglie ogni pensiero
alla mia testa e lo fa diventare
miele al cuore. Ma forse è una minestra
che ricadendo da una certa altezza
scioglie il mio corpo in tiepida emulsione:
tutto commosso corpo da trasporto
verso una lontanissima stazione.

Suddenly as if it were a cold
love is back. It's not a cold
it's a headache that takes away thought
in my head and turns it into
honey in my heart. But maybe it's a soup
that falling from a certain height
melts my body into a warm emulsion:
a body all moved being moved
towards a very distant hub.

GINI ALHADEFF

Piena di me gagliarda camminavo
sprezzantemente oltrepassavo il ponte,
diamante duro che ritagliava sguardi,
tirata asciutta nera crudelissima,
ah, che m'importa, mi dicevo, e tu,
prova a sfiorarmi!

Dietro due vecchie pazze rallentavo
e superata l'una mi trovai
tra quella che parlando s'ingombrava
e l'altra che in silenzio andava avanti.
Poi con furore intatto scavalcai
quegli smarriti intralci barcollanti.
Ma d'improvviso comparve una ragazza
al semaforo opposto, mendicante.
Una di fronte, le altre alle mie spalle,
mancando il verde decisi di guardarle.
E complicai il mio sguardo. Ero distante,
ma debolezza mi sbiancò le gambe.

I walked full of myself and very strong
crossing the bridge disdainfully
tough diamond sculpting the looks
taut tight black cruel
why should I care, I told myself, and you,
don't you dare even touch me!

Behind two crazy old women I slowed down
and overtaking one discovered myself
between a woman weighed down by talking
and another silently walking.
Then with untouched fury I went forward
past those lost lurching impediments.
Suddenly a girl appeared
at the streetlight across from me—a beggar.
One in front of me, the others behind,
the light wasn't green so I looked at them.
I complicated my sight. I was in the distance,
but weakness made my legs go white.

DAVID SHAPIRO WITH

GINI ALHADEFF

La stagione mi invita. Che stagione
è questa che mi invita? Ero sparita
nella piazza conclusa del mercato.
Il mercato scintilla ogni mattina
presto, ma poi la frutta si fa opaca,
frutta tardiva, io mi faccio strada,
il passo primavera stanco,
fra tutta quella merce che mi invita,
saluto e poi saluto e poi saluto
apro il cuore e la bocca e poi li chiudo,
il cuore si apre molto, anzi sale,
ah troppo sale e eccomi smarrita
dentro una lontanissima mattina,
pure così vicina, mia sorella
d'altri tempi gemella, eppure sempre
attenta, messe che curva cedevole
il suo dorso, che verso me si tende,
io non la colgo, e invece lei si ostina
a camminarmi accanto. È una mattina
di arrendevole luce, quasi vinta,
che quando non si vede s'indovina.
Ero in questa mattina e mi spargevo,
lo sguardo non bugiardo o veritiero
vedevo insieme felicità e rovina.

The season is inviting me. Which season is
inviting me? I'd disappeared
into the closed piazza of the marketplace.
The market glistens early every morning,
but then the fruit turns dark,
late fruit and I move ahead,
with my worn-out springtime step,
amidst all this merchandise that calls me,
I say hello and then hello and hello
I open heart and mouth and then I close them.
The heart opens a lot, it even rises,
ah it rises too far and here I am dismayed
inside a long-gone morning,
and yet so close, my sister,
twin of other times but always
present, harvest that generously bends
its back, that bends to me,
I don't take her and yet she insists
on walking with me. It's a morning
of surrendering light, almost defeated,
that when it isn't seen can be surmised.
I was in this morning and spread myself thin,
my look neither dishonest nor truthful,
and I saw both happiness and ruin.

JONATHAN GALASSI

Un respiro parziale ma intero
così nasce e si alza un pensiero,
mio pensiero parziale ma intero
così nasce così è.

One breath, partial but complete,
so it is a thought emerges, rises,
my thought, partial but complete,
so it is born, so it shall be.

JORIE GRAHAM

Cambiando posizione al tavolino
altro governo avrà il mio ragionare;
sarà più lento il passaggio al divano
dove sempre a ogni ostacolo dormivo.
Seduta, d'improvviso mi tuffavo
tra quei cuscini grandi e il mio pensiero
di sé sognando sciolto pascolava
fra tante erbette facili, qua e là.

If I turn my desk around
my thoughts will take a different tack;
the path to the sofa will be slower.
Before when I was stuck
I'd go to sleep without warning.
I'd plunge into the cushions and my thoughts,
dreaming themselves free, would graze
here and there among countless blades of grass.

MARK STRAND WITH

GINI ALHADEFF

Questi bei fasci di poesie che trovo
abbandonate al primo verso, o anche
al secondo, sono come le sciarpe
di Beau Brummell: gli insuccessi,
a sentire il cameriere. Però
non è soltanto il goffo primo gesto
che causa l'insuccesso, c'è nelle cose stesse
forse una svogliatezza a rivelarsi.
Si affacciano, ma poi, ostili, restano
così, senza spiegarsi. Anche a sforzarle
cadono male, non c'è maestria
che le potrà salvare.
(O pigrizia, come sei spirituale!)

These lovely sheaves of poetry I find
abandoned at the first line or the second
are like Beau Brummell's cravats:
the unsuccessful ones,
his valet says. And yet
it's not just the maladroit first gesture
that makes the failure, in the things themselves perhaps
is an unwillingness to be revealed.
They come to the window, but then, hostile, they remain
like this, won't open out. And if you force them
they end badly too, there's no art
that will save them.
(O laziness, how spiritual you are!)

JONATHAN GALASSI

Terapia

Ah, datemi una stanza in un albergo
una stanzetta una stanzetta in un albergo
sì, una stanza una stanza in un albergo
una stanzetta una stanzetta in un albergo . . .

(. . . e via così di seguito
senza fermarsi mai,
finché annoiati o esausti
si cade tramortiti
sopra un qualunque letto
anche se sfatto e lercio.)

Therapy

O give me a room in a hotel
a little room a little room in a hotel
yes, a room a room in a hotel
a little room a little room in a hotel.

(. . . and so it goes
without end,
until bored and exhausted
I fall half-dead
on any old bed
even unmade, even dirty.)

MARK STRAND

Quel che è perduto mi è restituito
quel che è lontano oggi mi è vicino.
Che tu ci sia, dove tu sia, oggi non importa,
oggi mi stringe la cupola dolcissima
inumidisce e impasta la matassa che sorge
dei rumori. Io sono dentro
e mi entra dentro il fuori.

What is lost is returned to me,
what is far away is near me today.
Whether you're here, wherever you are, doesn't matter today,
today I am held within a honeyed dome
that dampens and mingles the surging skein
of sounds. I am inside
and the outside enters me.

J. D. MCCLATCHY

from
pigre divinità
e pigra sorte ₂₀₀₆

from
lazy gods,
lazy fate ₂₀₀₆

Il mio paesaggio che credevo sconfinato
perché scomposto e ricomposto mi illudeva
di sempre nuovi boschi intricatissimi
di fitti prati mossi e inaspettati,
ora arrivata ai margini lo vedo: chiuso
orticello calpestato e spoglio, forse
per troppa cura soffocato. E allora

spoglia anch'io andrò nel ricco mondo, anche
se temo il suo ferroso chiasso. Che mi si spalmi
addosso, suderò sperduta, a me perduta,
di me ortolana io che me ne faccio?

Straniera arresa finalmente e penetrabile
mi do mi offro, no anzi raccolgo erbette
strane che mai avevo visto, e non farò
cataloghi scientifici, le annuserò soltanto
forse le mangio, venefiche o inebrianti
o senza esito, che importa, anche in ritardo
io qui mi schiudo al mio nuovo coraggio.

Aperto campo, da sempre ero invitata,
potevo andare, perché non sono andata?
Anche se poi mi pare, sì, ricordo,
sono sicura, io lì c'ero già stata.

My landscape, which I thought was limitless
because disassembled and put back together again it gave me the illusion
of always new most intricate forests
of dense meadows, ruffled and unexpected,
now having reached the edge I can see: a closed
little vegetable garden, walked on and bare,
suffocating perhaps by too much care. And so

bare myself I'll go into the unbroken world, even
though I fear its crashing noise. Let it spread
over me, I sweat and feel lost, lost to myself,
a greengrocer to me, what's the use of that?

I'm the stranger finally surrendering and penetrable
I give myself up I offer myself, no, in fact I pick up strange
grasses I'd never seen before, that I will not render
for scientific catalogues, I'll only sniff them
perhaps I'll eat them, poisonous, intoxicating,
or ineffectual, who cares, even this late
I open to my new audacity.

An open field, I'd always been invited,
I could have gone there, why didn't I?
Even though if I think of it, yes, I remember now,
I'm fairly certain I'd been there before.

DAVID SHAPIRO WITH

GINI ALHADEFF

Sto qui ci sono e faccio la mia parte.
Ma io neanche so cos'è questa mia parte.
Se lo sapessi
potrei almeno uscire dalla parte
e poi sciolta da me godermela in disparte.

Here I am, I do my bit,
though I don't know what that may be.
If I did I could at least let go of it
and free of it be free of being me.

GINI ALHADEFF

Chi entra in un vagone dà prova di se stesso,
tralascia il corpo, esercita lo spirito,
mette a dormire i sensi, dorme davvero
o li devia in un libro, in un giornale,
o fissa cieco un punto casuale
pur di non confondersi alla mischia.
Ma nella luce bianca
e cruda sono tutti uguali,
popoli perduti solo affidati
a ciò che una residua vista
potrebbe forse ancora intravedere
di quella strana sorprendente cosa
che un tempo, non tanto tempo fa,
era una faccia.

Whoever boards a train is tested,
neglects the body, trains the spirit,
puts the senses to sleep, really sleeps
or transfers them to a book, a newspaper,
or blindly stares at a casual spot   ·
anything not to mix with the crowd.
But in the white crude light
everyone is the same,
lost people simply offered up
to what any residual eyesight
might still glean perhaps
of that strange surprising thing
that once, not so long ago,
was a face.

GINI ALHADEFF

Piccione zoppo. Ridicolo
piccione zoppo e storto.
Se hanno difetti gli animali
subito somigliano agli umani.

Lame pigeon. Ridiculous
lame crooked pigeon.
When they have defects animals
suddenly resemble humans.

GINI ALHADEFF

Più ci si annoia e più ci si affeziona.
M'annoio tanto, non voglio più morire.

The more bored you are, the more attached you get.
I'm so bored, I no longer want to die.

GINI ALHADEFF

Pigre divinità e pigra sorte

Pigre divinità e pigra sorte
cosa non faccio per incoraggiarvi,
quante occasioni con fatica vi offro
solo perché possiate rivelarvi!
A voi mi espongo e faccio vuoto il campo
e non per me, non è nel mio interesse,
solo per farvi esistere mi rendo
facile visibile bersaglio. Vi do
anche un vantaggio, a voi l'ultima mossa,
io non rispondo, a voi quell'imprevisto
ultimo tocco, rivelazione
di potenza e grazia: ci fosse un merito
sarebbe solo vostro. Perché io non voglio
essere fabbrica della fortuna
mia, vile virtù operaia che
mi annoia. Avevo altre ambizioni, sognavo
altre giustizie, altre armonie: ripulse
superiori, predilezioni oscure,
d'immeritati amori regalíe.

Lazy Gods, Lazy Fate

Lazy gods, lazy fate
what don't I do to encourage you,
think of the chances I strain to offer you
just so you might appear!
I lay myself bare to you and clear the field
not for me, it's not in my interest,
just so you might exist I become
an easy visible target. I even give you
a handicap, to you the last move,
I won't respond, to you that unforeseen
last round, a revelation
of force and grace: if there were to be any merit
it would be yours alone. Because I don't want
to be the factory of my own fate,
cowardly workmanly virtue
bores me. I had different ambitions, dreamt
of other kinds of judgments, other harmonies: grander
rejections, obscure predilections,
the fringe benefits of undeserved love.

GINI ALHADEFF

Questo tempo sabbatico
prima di una partenza, questo tempo
rubato al tempo, questo tempo non mio
né di altri, il tempo della valigia
e del ritardo, questo lusso sospeso,
questo margine ricco,
quando audace e irresponsabile posso
quello che neanche gli anni mi concedono,
dove accorrono i pensieri più negletti
e sono accolti, e tra un pigiama
e una camicia s'insedia maestoso
ma arrendevole il possibile, dove potrei
persino telefonarti e dichiararmi
folle d'amore, questo unico tempo vero
involontario che ci è dato
per grazia di partenze, questo
non è nient'altro che preghiera.

This sabbatical time
before a departure, this time
stolen from time, this time not mine
or anyone else's, time of suitcases
and delays, suspended luxury,
generous margin,
when daring and irresponsible I can do
what my age wouldn't permit,
where the most neglected thoughts arise
and are accepted, and between pajamas and a shirt,
surrendering, majestically settles the possible,
where I might even phone you and declare myself
madly in love, this sole real
involuntary time which we are given
by the grace of departure, this
is nothing but prayer.

GINI ALHADEFF

per Alice Ceresa

Quasi sempre alla morte di qualcuno
che ci era caro e che però di rado
incontravamo, si pensa:—ma perché
non l'ho visto più spesso? Adesso non c'è più
e forse mai gli ho veramente detto
quanto l'ammiravo. Come è sciatto l'affetto
che non sa farsi visibile in un gesto!
Come in quei sogni dove arriva un bene
che è lì a due passi e non si sa godere.
E poi che spreco in ogni onore postumo,
in ogni lode o celebrazione.
Perché chi è morto ormai quale piacere
quale vantaggio ne potrebbe avere?
È tutto vero ma è un pensiero sciocco.
Essere in vita infatti non è altro
che il lusso di un ritardo, restare
nel possibile sospesi tra il poco
e il troppo, ma sempre fuori posto,
sentendo che si può,
che si potrebbe, in un fresco presente
immaginato, pascolo ricco
che viene tralasciato. Solo la morte,
che in sé è inesistente, rende assoluto
il tempo ormai concluso: a noi resta

for Alice Ceresa

Almost always when we hear that someone's died,
someone we liked but hardly ever took
the trouble to seek out, we think:—but why
didn't we meet more often? Now he's gone
and maybe I never really let him know
how much I admired him. It's a poor affection
that never becomes manifest in an act.
Like in those dreams when a longed-for good arrives
just at our fingertips, but we can't reach it.
And then, what a waste, every posthumous honor,
every slather of praise and celebration.
Because what possible pleasure or advantage
could someone dead derive from any of this?
All this is true, but it's a stupid thought.
Because being alive, in fact, is nothing but
the luxury of a delay, a dallying
in the possible, suspended between too little
and too much, but always out of place,
feeling that one can,
one might, in a juicy, imaginary present,
a fat and beckoning pastureland
now abandoned. Death alone,
that doesn't exist in itself, makes absolute
a time cut short: all we retain

il pensiero di chi è assente, fermo pensiero
stupefatto inerme, ché l'immaginazione
trova chiuso. Per questo si ricorre
alla memoria: quel che era mondo aperto
si fa storia e storia che si insedia
nella mente, perché chi non c'è più
sia finalmente sicura intatta
eternità presente.

is the thought of the absent one, a motionless
stunned and defenseless thought where imagination
cannot enter. That's why we fall back
on memory: what we once knew as an open world
becomes history, a history that settles
in the mind, so that the person no longer here
should be an ultimate assured intact
present eternity.

ROSANNA WARREN

Guarda!
Tutti vogliono essere guardati.
Anche chi si sottrae a ogni vista
vuole idealmente essere guardato.
Ma chi ha paura non vede e non è visto,
è la paura che arma gli assassini.
Guarda, sono già morta.
Guardami! Risorgimi!

Look!
Everyone wants to be looked at.
Even the one who withdraws from every gaze
wants to be seen in an ideal light.
But whoever is afraid can't see or be seen;
it's fear that arms assassins.
Look, I'm already dead.
Look at me! Revive me!

SUSAN STEWART AND
BRUNELLA ANTOMARINI

Ah resta dove sei! Io qui
nell'ora incerta di un tardo pomeriggio
guardando fuori e anche guardando dentro
vedo questa bellezza
tutto quello che vedo è la bellezza.
Qualcosa che convince, che vuole essere vista,
che pure non fa nulla, ma resta lì dov'è,
che solo perché esiste mi conquista.

O stay where you are! Here
in the uncertain hour of a late afternoon
looking outward and looking in
I see this beauty
all I see is beauty.
Something that convinces, asks to be seen,
though it does nothing, just stays where it is,
and merely by existing wins me over.

GINI ALHADEFF

Certo è ridicolo e forse scandaloso
che io provi così potente invidia
per quel figlio undicenne insonnolito
caduto tra le braccia di sua madre
a godersi il suo turno di piacere
per quanto inconsapevole e stordito.
Come potrei alla mia età competere
con quei capelli lievi, quella fronte
che si ritrae per farsi più cedevole
alla forza sicura delle mani
che la chiudono dentro le carezze,
non leziose carezze ma indiscussa
sovranità di asciutta tenerezza,
vera carezza certa che possiede?
Non trovo alcun rimedio alla mia invidia:
che cosa voglio io, dare o ricevere?
Essere quel che sono, eppure figlio,
non figlia femmina, ma femminile
figlio, figlio assoluto, imprecisato
figlio. Ah madre mia che avevo, perché
non mi hai convinto?

Surely it's ridiculous maybe even scandalous
that I feel such overpowering envy
for the eleven-year-old son who's dozing
fallen into his mother's arms
to enjoy his turn of pleasure
however unaware and heedless.
At my age how could I compete
with that fine hair, that brow
which pulls back all the better to surrender
to the sure power of those hands
that close him in their caresses,
not lustful caresses but undisputed
sovereignty of simple tenderness,
the true sure gesture that possesses?
There's no cure for my envy:
what do I want, to give or to receive?
To be what I am, yet not a female daughter
but a feminine son, an absolute son,
an undifferentiated son. Mother of mine,
what went wrong, why didn't you convince me?

JONATHAN GALASSI

Voglio il mio bene adesso cosa faccio?
Non so neanche da dove cominciare.
Perché ho quest'infallibile certezza
quando voglio raggiungere il mio male,
mentre per il mio bene non ho idea
non ho nessuna idea su cosa fare?
Forse perché il male è esuberanza
di spirito che anela a straripare
e uscendo poi dal margine rivela
eccesso di materia, dismisura
che si rovescia in varietà di forme,
dissonanza che esalta quel che c'è
non quel che manca. E dunque se lo cerco
io lo trovo, basta muoversi un po',
intraprendere, volere. Il bene essendo
invece assenza di sostanza, recede
da ogni forma e non si svela: quando lo cerco
diventa il suo fantasma, credo di averlo
e subito mi manca. Se allora
il male è un più e il bene un meno, come
posso volere, cosa spero? Ogni
mia volonta è perdizione. Perciò
dovrei restare dove sono, senza
mente ambiziosa, ma innocente
di tutto, anche del bene,
a questo anzi ritrosa.

I want my own good, what can I do about it?
I don't even know how or where to begin.
Why does an unshakeable certitude seize on me
whenever I desire to grasp my ill,
whereas about my good, I've no idea,
not the slightest idea of what to do?
Maybe because ill is all exuberance
of spirit that swells to overflowing,
and, leaping beyond its banks, reveals
excess of matter, total lack of measure
which spills out in a multitude of forms,
a dissonance exalting all that is,
and not what's missing. So if I look for it,
I find it, just by moving around a bit,
exerting myself, wanting it. Whereas the good,
being an absence of substance, withdraws
from every form and hides: when I look for it,
good becomes its own ghost, I think I've caught it,
and suddenly it vanishes. If then
ill is a more and good a less, how can
I want anything, what can I hope for? Every
longing brings damnation. Thus it's clear
I ought to stay quiet here where I am, without
a clamoring mind, but innocent
of everything, even of the good,
even resistant to it.

ROSANNA WARREN

Ogni bella giornata di novembre
è quasi sempre un'occasione persa.
La luce ha fretta
la luce di novembre non aspetta,
ci pensi sopra e non è più in offerta.
E ci si illanguidisce alla promessa
di una felicità, ah, più che certa
se solo avessi avuto l'accortezza
di predisporre il giusto materiale:
un giro inconcludente in bicicletta
e labbra sfaccendate da baciare.

Every fair November day
is almost always a missed opportunity.
The light is in a hurry
November light won't wait
you think it over and it's gone.
And I grow languid with the promise
of a happiness, well, more than certain
if only I'd had the foresight
to prepare the right equipment:
an aimless bike ride
and fallow lips for kissing.

GINI ALHADEFF

L'aria odorava di fuoco appena spento,
fuoco di carta o di paglia, forse di legno,
fuoco però domestico
anche se si spargeva in tutta la città
nel vecchio centro.
Non essere felici dentro quell'aria
pareva un sacrilegio. Il solito rumore
si acquietava, la strada
che mi portava a casa era nel giusto,
deserta per un po' e poi animata.
Non era caldo, ma non era freddo.
Sembrava primavera. Anzi lo era.

The air smelled of a fire that had just gone out,
burnt paper or straw, maybe wood,
a fire in a house somewhere
even though it spread everywhere
in the old city center.
To not be contented inside that air
seemed sacrilege. The usual noise
died down, the road
that took me home was just right,
deserted for a bit then animated.
It wasn't hot, it wasn't cold.
It might have been spring. In fact was.

GINI ALHADEFF

Cado e ricado, inciampo e cado, mi alzo
e poi ricado, le ricadute sono
la mia specialità. Cos'altro ho fatto
che fingere di uscire e ricadere dentro?
Nessuno mai che io trascini insieme a me
cadendo. Grandi equilibri mi circondano
ma non mi reggono, anzi proprio perché io cado
si sorreggono. Com'era bella la coppia
di vecchi innamorati che sottobraccio
volendo misurarsi per duplice entusiasmo
con la catena che chiude Ponte Sisto,
sicuri che quel restare insieme li avrebbe
sostenuti, caddero invece insieme
ancora sottobraccio, non umiliati
ma certo stupefatti di come quello stare
perfettamente in due li avesse sbilanciati,
e però grati comunque l'uno all'altro
di essere in due, che nessuno dei due
vedesse, l'uno salvo, cadere l'altro.

I fall and fall again, stumble and fall, get up
then fall again, relapses are
my specialty. What have I done
if not pretend to clamber out only to fall back in?
There's never anyone I drag along with me
when I fall. Great balance surrounds me
but doesn't hold me up, in fact it is because I fall
that others stand. How wonderful the couple
of old lovers who arm in arm
wanting by a double dare to test
the chain that seals off Ponte Sisto,
certain that their holding on to each other
would hold them up, fell together instead
still arm in arm, not humiliated
but certainly dumbstruck by how their being
perfectly paired had made them lose their balance
yet grateful to one another
that they were two, that neither of the two
while safe saw the other fall.

GINI ALHADEFF

Butta la pasta, arrivo!
Ah che gioia, mi dànno da mangiare.
L'acqua però non bolle, non ancora.
Che qualcuno stia lì a scaldare
l'acqua e poi arrivare in tempo
prima che la pasta scuocia
o che magari sia diventata fredda,
in quel momento esatto sempre
un po' isterico, sì proprio in quel momento
quasi sacro della scolatura,
questa fretta felice prima o poi,
anche ai più disgraziati, a tutti tocca.

Throw in the pasta, I'm on my way!
O bliss, I'll be fed.
But the water doesn't boil, not yet.
For someone to be there bringing
water to a boil and to get there on time
before the pasta overcooks
or God forbid grows cold,
in that exact always slightly hysterical
moment, yes, in that almost sacred
very moment of straining,
that happy haste sooner or later,
will come to all, even the unluckiest.

GINI ALHADEFF

Eravamo tutti perdonati.
Perché l'aria ci assorbiva
nella sua temperatura. La testa
piegata di lato, la guancia che tocca
la spalla e quasi l'accarezza. Liscio
il respiro, sollevato volante.
Il cuore pattinava controvento.
Oh varietà! Oh insieme!
Ogni strada è felice
se una pioggetta tiepida
intimidisce la luce
e la costringe a spargersi
senza predilezioni.
Più che perdono. Eravamo accolti.

We were all forgiven.
Because the air absorbed us
in its climate. The head
cocked to the side, the cheek touching
a shoulder and almost caressing it. The breath
was smooth, lifted up in flight.
The heart skated against the wind.
O variety! O togetherness!
Each street is happy
if a mild drizzle
overwhelms the light
and makes it scatter
any which way.
More than forgiven. We were welcome.

SUSAN STEWART AND

BRUNELLA ANTOMARINI

Guardare la bellezza e mai farla propria.
Se non fosse così guarderesti te stessa
non avresti cioé più nulla da guardare,
possidente annoiata di una noia lupesca.

To look at beauty and never make it yours.
If it weren't this way you'd look at yourself
that is, you'd have nothing more to look at,
bored possessor of a wolfish boredom.

GEOFFREY BROCK

Sono diventata molto saggia
dico saggezze una dietro l'altra
facilmente molto facilmente
le dico e le dimentico
posso dimenticarle
perché ne ho sempre un'altra.
D'altronde io
non sono mica il tipo che risparmia!

I've become very wise
I say wise things one after the other
easily very easily
I say them and forget them
I can forget them
because I'll always have another.
After all I
was never one to economize!

GINI ALHADEFF

Sempre voler capire. Non si può.
Bisogna cedere, bisogna ritirarsi,
bisogna fare come fanno i gatti
quando si acquattano, i muscoli in un fremito
contratti, prima di scagliarsi verso
una qualche preda, che sia per gioco
o che sia roba seria; o quando in ferocissimo
kabuki affrontano il rivale, e l'universo
intero allora si concentra in un assorto
e millimetrico avanzare, e poi
senza preavviso, forse perché si sta mettendo
male—la scusa è sempre una mosca o un moscerino
che si ritrova dalle loro parti—
guardano in giro, si fingono distratti,
loro che c'entrano? mica era sul serio!
Ma chissà, forse si distraggono davvero.

Always wanting to understand. You can't.
You have to yield, you have to retreat,
you have to do what cats do
when they crouch, that shudder of muscles
contracting before they hurl themselves towards
some prey or other, maybe playfully,
maybe meaning business; or when in the fiercest
Kabuki they confront a rival, and the whole
universe distills into a single-minded
millimetric advance, and then
without warning, perhaps because things are looking
bad—the excuse is always some fly or gnat
discovered in their vicinity—
they look around, pretend to be distracted,
what has this to do with them? it was hardly serious!
But who knows, maybe they really do get distracted.

GEOFFREY BROCK

Le strade sono calde, le voci ingombrano,
è marzo ormai, di nuovo marzo come
fosse ieri, i morti avanzano,
anzi scompaiono. Troppi morti infatti
e non c'è neanche guerra,
morti perché si muore.

The streets are hot, the voices in the way,
it's March now, March again
like it was yesterday, the dead are advancing,
indeed vanishing. Too many dead in fact
and not even a war on,
dead because we die.

GEOFFREY BROCK

Ah, ma è evidente, muoio.
Sto per morire, che siano giorni
o anni, sto per morire,
muoio. Lo fanno tutti,
dovrò farlo anch'io. Sì, mi conformo
alla regola banale. Però intanto,
tra un sonno e l'altro finché esiste il sonno
(solo chi è in vita gode del suo sonno)
guardando il cielo, girando gli occhi
intorno, in questi istanti incerti
io sono certamente un'immortale.

It's pretty clear, I'm dying
I'm about to die, in a matter of days
or years, I'm about to die,
I'm dying. Everyone does it,
I'll have to do it, too. Yes, I must conform
to that humdrum law. But in the meantime,
between one sleep and another as long as there is sleep
(only the living can enjoy sleep)
looking at the sky, rolling my eyes
in those uncertain moments
I am most certainly immortal.

GINI ALHADEFF

per Annalisa

Come fatica la vita! Sa
di dover finire, è condannata,
e anche nel morire si affatica.
Pure diminuita, eccola che si ostina
a fare la sua parte, a far la vita.

for Annalisa

How life tries! It knows
it must end, it's condemned,
and even in dying it tries.
Even diminished, there it is, it persists,
playing its part, playing at life.

GINI ALHADEFF

Incapace d'amore, Amore Fisiologico
con i più bassi mezzi mi tortura.
Ha a sua disposizione la vastità del corpo
reso ancora più vasto dal dolore.
Il sangue raspa e preme contro vene
e arterie e l'osso sterno che ripara
il cuore si sbriciola in acri trafitture.
Un sodalizio di lacrime e languore
si addensa nella zona occipitale
mentre una lama attraversa la cervice
e scende lunga quanto la dorsale.
Filo spinato elettrificato
penetra il manto della pia madre
e sparge scariche nel lobo temporale.
Il nervo vago ormai terrorizzato
lascia le redini e imbizzarisce il cuore.
La linfa senza ordini e governo
non riesce più a fare il suo viaggio
si ferma sui binari dove capita
o ingorga le stazioni ghiandolari.
Solo terrore c'è e solo smarrimento.
E tutto questo per farmi confessare
che io non sono in nessun modo mai spirituale.

Incapable of love, Physiological Love
tortures me by the basest of means.
It has at its disposal the vastness of the body
rendered even vaster by pain.
Blood rushes and presses against veins
and arteries, and the sternum that shelters
the heart shatters into sharp spurs.
A sodality of tears and languor
gathers in the occipital zone
while a blade pierces the cervix
and descends all down the backbone.
Barbed wire electrified
penetrates the mantle of the pia mater
and sends shocks into the temporal lobe.
The vagus nerve by now terrorized
drops the reins and frenzies the heart.
Lymph without orders, ungoverned,
no longer can make its journey
stops along the tracks wherever
or jams the glandular terminals.
Nothing but terror is there and dismay.
And all this just to make me admit
that I am in no way ever spiritual.

GINI ALHADEFF

Amore non è vero che svolazza,
sta fermo e dorme invisibile nascosto
in caldo ripostiglio, il nostro corpo.
Ma quale sia precisamente il posto
finché sta fermo nessuno può saperlo,
quello che sceglie non è per tutti uguale.
Io certo non lo sveglio, però smania nel sonno
e so che adesso si è messo di traverso
proprio in quel punto dove mi fa male,
dietro la quarta vertebra dorsale.

It isn't true that Cupid flits about,
he stays put and sleeps invisible and hidden
in that cozy cubbyhole, our body.
But what his spot might be
as long as he stays put no one can know,
the one he picks is not the same for all.
I certainly won't be the one to wake him, but he's been fussing in his sleep
and I know he just stretched sideways
right there where it hurts,
behind the fourth vertebra of my spine.

GINI ALHADEFF

Il cielo anche oggi è azzurro
ma poi si sporca per le nuvole nascoste
dietro i palazzi più alti delle mie finestre.
Luce che si muove e muove ombre,
vuoto lentamente attraversato
da pigre ombre. Lo stanco repertorio
dei miei nervi insiste in repliche
che io più non guardo, che non ascolto,
non durano abbastanza da tenerne
conto. Ma intatta ancora regna in me
fisiologia, e mi costringe al sogno:
guarigione: regalo di endorfine
da te, la mia robiera. Non in regalo,
anzi te le pago, le pago cento volte
il loro prezzo. Tutto si compra e io
perché non posso? In questo mondo fatto
di rimedi, perché il mio rimedio
io non l'ottengo? Perché volere te
come rimedio? Perché se le tue labbra
si dischiudono quando distesa ti decidi
al bene e a consonanti doppie dici amore
non più alteramente casta ma
tutta assorta a bere il mio fervore,
perché allora il mio sangue si dispone
così armonioso e liscio nelle vene
e porta il miele all'orfana, la testa?

The sky is blue again today
but then it's soiled by clouds hiding
behind buildings taller than my windows.
Light that moves and moves the shadows,
a void that's slowly crossed
by lazy shadows. The tired repertory
of my nerves puts on performances
I no longer watch, no longer listen to,
they don't last long enough to
count. But in me physiology
still reigns intact, and forces me to dream:
the cure: an offer of endorphins
from you who are my pusher. Not as a gift,
because I'll pay a hundred times
their price—everything's for sale
so why shouldn't I? In this world made up
of remedies, why can't I get
mine? Why should one want you
for a remedy? Why if your lips
part when, lying down, you opt
for the good and in double vowels say
I love you, no longer proudly chaste but
all absorbed in drinking up my fervor,
why does my blood decide to flow then
harmonious and smooth along the veins
carrying honey to my orphan head?

GINI ALHADEFF

Le tasche

Sarebbe un'altra cosa la mia vita
se quel che mi circonda e mi accompagna
fosse disposto a gentile somiglianza
dei miei bisogni. Avrei la mia riuscita.

Le tasche, per esempio, sì, le tasche.
Le tasche sono sempre troppo basse.
Io camminando cerco il loro fondo
e per trovarlo mi chino m'arrotondo

molle alle spalle e vado giù costretta
a perlustrare il fetido selciato
orribile di Roma a valli e a dossi,
paurosa geografia dell'incertezza;

quei sampietrini ormai sempre sconnessi
in tante larghe tenebre, reticoli
dove ogni cosa sembra che precipiti.

Fossero invece alte e laterali,
le mani troverebbero un appoggio
costringendo le spalle ad arretrare.
E così, dritta, perpendicolare,

sarei fornita di quel passo ardito
che per precognizione scansa e aggira
i vetri di birrette e le cacate
di cani ipernutriti, gigantesche.

Pockets

How different my life would be
if all that surrounds me and is with me
were inclined to gently resemble
my needs. I'd have it made.

Pockets, for instance, yes, pockets.
Pockets are always placed too low.
Walking along I look for where they end
and to do so bend and round my back

shoulders drooping I sag, obliged
to survey the foul dread Roman
pavements all ditches and mounds,
a frightful geography of uncertainty;

those cobblestones now always disconnected
in so many gaping shadows, grids
in which everything appears to sink.

If they were placed high and on the side, instead,
the hands would find a resting place
forcing the shoulders to retreat.
And thus, upright, perpendicular,

I'd be equipped with a bold gait
that presciently dodges and circles
beer bottle shards and overfed dogs'
gigantic turds.

E sorvolando baratri e immondezze
guarderei avanti, e a sinistra e a destra,
con benevoli sguardi trascorrenti
a mezza altezza, dove c'è più offerta.

Ma io avrei fretta, perché il mio passo ormai
velocemente arioso lungimíra
la sua stazione vera, quella meta
dove pagando un dazio c'è la febbre.

Avrei una meta anch'io
dunque ho una meta.
O almeno sembrerebbe.

And skipping across chasms and trash
I'd look ahead, and to the left and to the right,
with benevolent passing glances
at midrange, where there's more on offer.

But I'd be in a hurry, because my gait by now
swift and breezy, looks ahead
to its true haven,
where if you pay the toll you'll get a fever.

And so I too would have a goal
I have a goal, then.
Or so it would seem.

GINI ALHADEFF

Ah mangiare i mandarini
che mai sanno di morte!

O to eat tangerines
that never taste of death!

GINI ALHADEFF

La guardiana

I

Era il sospetto del tuo chiuso ardore
che mi faceva artefice di chiavi.
D'altronde ero famosa da bambina
per aprire cassetti, porte e armadi
di cui non si trovava più la chiave.

Prima lasciavo che si presentassero
i competenti, ossia gli adulti maschi,
e io in silenzio buona da una parte
con noia superiore li guardavo
affaticarsi su quella serratura
che mai avrebbero aperto, ero sicura.
Dopo mezz'ora di maneggiamenti
aspri e stizzosi senza risultato,
quando alla fine si invocava il fabbro,
come un eroe in disuso risorgevo
flemmatica dicendo: l'apro io.

Con dei ferretti storti, mia invenzione,
a occhi semichiusi raggiungevo
il punto esatto, la prima tenerezza
nel dente dello scatto—tesa all'ascolto
tremante che pregavo. Ah il terrore
che potesse negarsi alla mia mano!

The Keeper

I

It was the thought of your locked-up heat
that made me into a wizard of keys.
After all I was famous as a child
for opening drawers, doors and cupboards
to which the key could no longer be found.

First I let the experts show up—
the grown-up males,
and quietly from the side
watched with superior boredom
as they labored over the lock
which they'd never unlock, I was sure.
After half an hour they'd fumbled
embittered and irate at not having succeeded
when in the end a locksmith was invoked
like a hero in disuse I rose up
phlegmatic, saying: I'll open it.

Using bent wires, my invention,
eyes half-closed I reached
the exact spot, the first yielding
in the tooth of the lock—
straining to hear, trembling, I prayed.
O the terror that my hand might meet refusal!

Ma quale comunione, quando ormai dentro
tutta trasferita, sentendo che era
intimamente mia, con un colpo
leggero la guidavo e lei senza resistere
si apriva. Non so come facessi, ero ispirata,
non era scienza, era devozione.

Nessun mistero si apriva a quella porta,
era una porta una qualsiasi porta
e nel cassetto c'era quel che c'era,
ognuno lo sapeva. E delle lodi,
unico premio alla mia impresa, molte
all'inizio, via via sempre più scarse
—la mia bravura col tempo era scontata—
di quelle poco o niente mi importava.
Il mio piacere era tutto nella sfida
di poter sciogliere quell'ostinato
inaccessibile diniego dove
nient'altro io ero che lo strumento eletto
per la resa: recedere di forze
entrando senza forza, solo ascoltando,
indifferente al premio ed al guadagno,
il suono che si leva da ogni chiusa
materia, che non aspetta altro
che aprirsi e darsi in dono
ma solo a chi è già pronto per quel suono.
Con quei ferretti storti, poi parole,
mi stavo esercitando alla poesia.
Che cosa'altro sennò? Sì, stavo imparando.

But what communion, once having entered
entirely moved in, feeling it to be
intimately mine, with a light
tap I guided it and offering no resistance
it opened. I don't know how I did it, I was inspired,
it wasn't science, it was devotion.

No mystery lay beyond that door,
it was a door a door like any other
and in the drawer was whatever was there,
everyone knew. And as to praises,
the only reward for my feats, many
at first, then fewer and fewer
—my prowess, with time, was taken for granted—
I cared little or nothing at all.
My pleasure lay only in the challenge
of unraveling that obstinate
inaccessible resistance to which
I was only the chosen instrument
of surrender: forces withdrawn
entering without forcing, only listening,
indifferent to the prize and to the profit,
the sound that rises from every sealed
thing, waiting just
to open and give itself away
but only to one ready for that sound.
With those bent wires, then words,
I practiced poetry.
What else if not that? Yes, I was learning.

Perché poi il tradimento? Com'è che poi tradii
insieme alla mia infanzia l'ozioso suo talento?
Cresciuta infatti, molto cresciuta, pratica
e impaziente, grave di scopi, gonfia
di mete, io come quegli adulti affaticati
affaticandomi ostinatamente
smaniosa sempre di aprire e di raggiungere
il tesoro nascosto, le delizie in maschera,
perduta la felice noncuranza,
l'indifferenza al premio, cercavo solo premi
e ricompense, beh sì, la mia spettanza.
Ah quante porte c'erano chiuse per me da aprire!
Non più fornita di chiavi celesti
divenni dunque artefice in carriera
di chiavi d'altro tipo, s'intende,
chiavi false: perché—io ragionavo—
se scrigno e cassaforte chiudono soldi e oro
allora anche le porte difficili da aprire,
sia pure d'altro genere, nascondono un tesoro.

Ah quante porte aprii, cassetti e pure
armadi! E che trovavo?
Una saletta riscaldata al minimo
da dove si accedeva a una cucina
tutta al risparmio, le luci poche e stente,
cibo scadente ma tre televisori.
Una famiglia vera e propria insomma
e se non questa, ricordi di famiglia
e se non questi, progetti di famiglia.
Giusto mezz'ora e me ne andavo via.

Why the betrayal, then? How was it I betrayed
along with my childhood its slothful talent, too?
Growing up, very grown up, practical
and impatient, laden with purpose, inflated
with goals, like those tired adults
tiring obstinately
ever eager to open and to reach
hidden treasures, masked delights,
having lost my blissful nonchalance
an indifference to prizes, I sought nothing but prizes
and rewards, well, yes, my due.
O how many doors there were for me to open!
No longer equipped with celestial keys
I became a professional wizard
of another kind of key, of course,
false keys: because—I told myself—
if vaults and safes lock away money and gold
then even hard-to-open doors,
including those of another kind, must hide a treasure.

O how many doors I opened, drawers and cupboards,
too! And what did I find?
A room with the heat turned low
that led into a penny-pinching
kitchen, with few lights on and feeble,
second-rate food but three television sets.
A proper family in fact
and if not that, memories of a family
and if not those, plans for a family.
Just half an hour then I'd go.

Eppure lo sapevo, lo sapevo
che a quella porta non si apriva alcun mistero,
era una porta una qualsiasi porta
e nel cassetto c'era quel che c'era,
e non soltanto io, chiunque lo sapeva.

Però non mi arrendevo: a stare lì
da sola fuori al freddo a far su e giù
su quel mio acerbo pascolo. Dovrà
pur esserci il sontuoso caldo
e straripanti tavole di cibo
mentre si gioca seri al Vero e al Falso.
Sì, ma dov'era il sontuoso caldo,
la luce ardente che mozza lo sguardo,
la lenta cerimonia che solenne accoglie
il tempestoso viaggiatore stanco?
Dov'erano le offerte di cuscini
su cui assorbire in silenzio il cibo santo?

Qual era quella porta? Se c'era io l'avrei aperta.

II

L'aria era dolce e molto profumata
di erbe e sale che il caldo aveva munto,
era di sera a cena un fine luglio
su una terrazza che pretendeva al mare.
Un golf a righe legato sulle spalle

Though I knew, knew
that that door opened on no mystery,
it was a door a door like any other
and in the drawer was whatever was there,
and I wasn't the only one to know, everyone did.

Still I didn't give up—staying out there
alone in the cold going up and down
that meager pasture of mine. Sumptuous
heat must exist somewhere
and tables overflowing with food
as the game of True and False is gravely played.
Yes, but where was the sumptuous heat,
the glowing light that blunts the gaze,
the slow ceremony that solemnly greets
the roaming weary traveler?
Where was the proffering of pillows
from which to silently absorb the blessed food?

What door was that? Had it been there I would have opened it.

II

The air was sweet and very scented
with grasses and salt the heat had milked out,
it was night, around dinnertime, at the end of July
on a terrace straining towards the sea.
A striped sweater tied around her shoulders

apparve lenta e scura la Guardiana.
La riconobbi subito: sprezzante
non salutò, non si presentò.
Padrona dei suoi passi, malinconica,
in ritardo, fortificata e accorta:
l'immobile, severa, inalterabile
Guardiana della Porta.
Se questa è la guardiana, mi dicevo,
chissà cosa nasconde la sua porta.
Perché, è evidente, si fa guardia inflessibile
solo a una porta che ha serratura debole
e che rivelerebbe, aprendosi, delizie
talmente ineludibili e fatali
che anche la guardia ne sarebbe persa.

Come quando in zone buie e solitarie
tornando soli senza voglia al proprio albergo
—è di notte per giunta e fa un po' freddo—
da una finestra appena aperta su un giardino
esce una vampa di luci e di risate
—perché ridono tanto? chi ci sarà là dentro?—
e pensi che meglio di come stanno loro
non si potrebbe stare in quel momento
e pagheresti pur di poter entrare
nelle radiosa radura della stanza;
o come quando a fine mattinata
andando frettolosi per faccende
da una cucina che affaccia sulla strada
esce un soffritto dolce di carne e di cipolle

slow and dark the Keeper appeared.
I recognized her right away: aloof
she did not say hello, or introduce herself.
In command of her steps, melancholic,
late, buttressed and vigilant:
the unmoving, stern, immutable
Keeper of the Door.
If this is the keeper, I told myself,
who knows what lies beyond her door.
Because, it's obvious, one guards inflexibly
only a door that has a feeble lock
and that would reveal, when opened, delights
so encompassing and fatal
even the keeper might fall prey to them.

As when in dark and solitary neighborhoods
returning listlessly to one's hotel alone
—it's night, what's more, and a little cold—
from a window barely open onto a garden
a burst of light and laughter escapes
—why are they laughing so? who are those people?
and you think no one could be better off
than they at that moment
and you'd pay to be admitted
to the radiant clearing of the room;
as when at morning's end,
while you rush through errands,
from a kitchen facing the street
a sweet smell of frying onions and meat escapes

e pensi che se non proprio a pranzo tu lì
a mangiare prima o poi ci andrai senz'altro
e già non vedi l'ora che arriverà quel giorno,
così da lei sarebbe uscita, se socchiusa,
una tale promessa di piaceri
che lo spiraglio era già un ricco acconto.
A aprirla tutta, che cosa avrei trovato!

I baci lunghi e il mare
languidamente inerme, addormentato, e braccia
piene di spazio, immense, e i golfi
quasi di latte, fermi, di settembre; e io nuotavo
in quella densa superficie e la parte
di me che stava emersa al sole si scaldava
per poi riimmergersi nell'acqua a farsi fresca.

Pertanto ciondolavo, le ciondolavo intorno
come un ladro, saggiando il territorio
dov'era molle, più facile allo scavo:
sforzando al massimo il mio usato repertorio
tentavo di distrarla dal suo compito,
che forse distraendosi mi mostra
come arrivare alla Sublime Porta.
Bisognava trovarla, ero un'esperta,
fosse pure blindata, magari con la forza,
io l'avrei aperta.

Allora non sapevo che c'era la guardiana,
soltanto la guardiana e non la porta,
una guardiana che allude ad una porta

and you think though not for lunch perhaps
but sooner or later you'll definitely eat there
and you can't wait for the day when it comes,
and from that door, too, would have escaped, had it been ajar,
such a promise of pleasures
that the breach alone would have been generous down payment.
Opening it all the way, what would I have found!

Long kisses and the sea
languidly inert, asleep, and arms
full of space, immense, September gulfs
almost milky, and still; and I swam
in that dense surface and the part
of me that emerged was warmed in the sun
then re-immersed itself in the water to be cooled.

And so I hung around, hung around her
like a thief, testing the ground
where it was soft, easier to excavate:
stretching my hackneyed repertory to the limit
I tried to distract her from her task,
so that once distracted she might show me
how to reach the Door Sublime.
It had to be found, I was an expert,
and armored or not, possibly by force
I'd open it.

I didn't know then that there was a keeper,
just the keeper and no door,
a keeper alluding to a door,

meravigliosa e forse facile da aprire,
basta saperlo fare, non certo con la forza.
Mi offriva intanto porticine laterali
che davano su bassi scantinati
due per quattro, nei quali avrei dovuto fare
mostra di tutti i numeri del mio gran varietà.
Ma ti lamenti troppo—mi diceva—
e poi non sai ballare, lo vedi, hai il gesto goffo
hai rotto due bicchieri. Ah no, non ti ci porto,
no, io a palazzo non ti faccio entrare.
E cominciai il mio balletto zoppo.

III

Quando io svegliandomi al mattino entravi
nella costituzione dei pensieri
che in fraseggio infinito compitavano
gli enigmi da risolvere, i sacrifici e i doni
che avrei deposto sulla soglia stretta
del tuo così diversamente ingombro
mattino di fretta e di faccende, da cui
usciva, senza che mai davvero io
la vedessi, quel solito rumore
di porta che si chiude, disperando
di me ostinata artefice di deluse chiavi,
cercavo la mia perduta grazia, quell'infanzia
che in armonia cedevole ascoltava.
Ero colpevole. Di non saper raggiungere
per troppa mira la chiusa morbidezza

wondrous even easy to open,
if you knew how, never using force.
She offered me small side doors, meanwhile,
opening onto dank basements
two meters by four, in which I'd have to
show off all the numbers in my variety show.
Well, you complain too much—she said—
and you can't even dance, see—you're clumsy
you broke two glasses. Oh no, I'm not taking you there,
forget the palace—I'm not letting you in.
And so I began my hobbling dance.

III

When in the morning I awoke and you entered
the constitution of thoughts
that in infinite phrasings spelled out
the engimas to be solved, the sacrifices and gifts
I would lay on the narrow threshold
of your so differently encumbered
morning of haste and tasks from which
proceeded, without my ever
having seen it, the usual sound
of a door shutting, giving up
on me, obstinate wizard of disappointed keys,
I searched for my lost grace, that infancy
which in yielding harmony listened.
I was guilty. Of not being able to reach
for having aimed too straight at it the cloistered softness

del tuo cuore: passando per la mente,
sì, con le parole, le valorose mie nobili
scudiere, cui avevo sempre dato
immenso credito—che a loro era passata
la gloria delle chiavi. E adesso che cos'erano
se non le vuote prove di un avvocato
che voglia impratichirsi del mestiere?
Un'impotente e macchinosa avvocatura
per rendermi ai tuoi occhi, e ai miei,
meno colpevole. Di non saper trovare
la porta che non c'era, quella sognata porta
che ti chiudeva centuplicata in bene,
che anche tu, guardiana stanca, sapevi
che non c'era, ma che anche tu sognavi,
sperando che le chiavi, la faticosa
virtù delle mie chiavi facesse esistere
quello che non c'era, che se io avessi inventato
il suono giusto, il giusto combinarsi
di parole, fossi riuscita nella
descrizione, saremmo entrate in due
in quell'invenzione. Per poi scoprire
che il piacere non ha porte e che
se mai l'avesse stanno aperte, che
potevamo allora rimanere fuori
sfornite e arrese tutte e due alla pari
giocando io alla porta e tu alle chiavi.

of your heart: passing through the mind,
yes, with words, my valiant noble
squires, to which I'd always given
great credit—since on them had been conferred
the glory of the keys. And now what were they
but the vain rehearsals
of an attorney learning his trade?
A hopeless trumped-up plea
to make me seem in your eyes, and mine,
less culpable. Of not being able to find
the door that wasn't there, the dreamed-of door
that locked you away in goodness multiplied,
which even you, tired keeper, knew
was not there, but which even you dreamed of,
hoping that the keys, the laborious
virtue of my keys, could bring into existence
what wasn't there, for if only I had found out
the right sound, the right combination
of words, managed the right
description, we might both have entered
into that invention. To finally discover
that pleasure has no doors and that
if it does they're wide open, and
that we could have stayed outside
both of us ill-equipped and surrendering equally
playing at door and keys
with me as the door and you as the keys.

GINI ALHADEFF

Essere animale per la grazia
di essere animale nel tuo cuore.
Mi scorge amore, mi scorge quando dormo.
Per questo io dormo. Di solito io dormo.

To be animal for the grace
of being animal in your heart.
Love sees me, sees me while I sleep.
It's why I sleep. Usually I sleep.

GINI ALHADEFF

Amore non mio e neanche tuo
ma chiuso prato dove siamo entrate,
da dove poco dopo sei riuscita
e dove io infingarda ho fatto casa.
Io guardo te da dentro che stai fuori,
che gironzoli ai margini distratta
e a volte ti avvicini a controllare
se ancora sono lì ferma e stordita.

Love not mine not yours,
but the fenced-in field that we entered
from which you soon moved out
and where I'd lazily made my home.
I watch you from the inside, you out there,
strolling distracted on the outskirts
and coming closer now and then to check
whether I'm still there, stopped and stunned.

MOIRA EGAN AND

DAMIANO ABENI

Diventai buona. E buona buona
facevo pascolare il disamore.
Su mangia questo, gli dicevo, che t'ingrassi,
no quello non toccarlo, che ti svuota.
Per dargli il buon esempio io stessa
m'ingrassai, e tutti e due
molto soddisfatti occupavamo placidi
i giorni e le stagioni. Ma poi, si sa,
la pace ti sfinisce: grassi e sfiniti, questo
è proprio il colmo! D'estate soprattutto,
l'estate ardimentosa.

Come lo sciolgo, come lo anniento
quel parassita torpido che ormai
si è abituato a credersi il padrone?
Venite predatori, mangiate le sue carni,
fatele a pezzi, lui si è preso sul serio,
distruggetelo! Io no, fingevo, io fingevo,
io posso dimagrirmi quando voglio,
guardate, sono già magra.

I became good. And like a goody-goody
I took unlove out to pasture.
Go on, eat this up, I'd say, it'll fatten you up,
as for that, don't touch it, it'll empty you out.
To give a good example I myself
got fat, and both of us
much satisfied placidly occupied
the days and seasons. But then, everyone knows,
peace does you in: fat and undone, it's
really the end! In the summer especially,
the surviving summer.

How can I melt it, how can I murder it
that sleepy parasite who by now
is used to believing he's the boss?
Come killers, eat his flesh,
tear it to pieces, he took himself seriously,
exterminate him! Not me, I was faking, faking,
I'll thin myself down whenever I want.
Look, I'm already thin.

DAVID SHAPIRO WITH
GINI ALHADEFF

Bene, vediamo un po' come fiorisci,
come ti apri, di che colore hai i petali,
quanti pistilli hai, che trucchi usi
per spargere il tuo polline e ripeterti,
se hai fioritura languida o violenta,
che portamento prendi, dove inclini,
se nel morire infradici o insecchisci,
avanti su, io guardo, tu fiorisci.

So, let's see how you flower,
how you open up, the color of your petals,
how many pistils you have, what tricks you use
to scatter pollen and replicate yourself,
whether your blossoming is languid or violent,
what posture you take, where you lean,
if while dying you dry up or go sour:
come on now, I look, you flower.

MOIRA EGAN AND

DAMIANO ABENI

Amore mi vinceva
vinceva non la forza
perché non ero forte
ma debole e già vinta.
Amore mi stringeva
sarebbe stato forte
ma non era, non era
forte amore, era però
signore.

Love was winning me over
it didn't win my strength
because I wasn't strong
I was weak, defeated.
Love gripped me
it might have been strong
but it wasn't, wasn't
strong love, but
lordly.

DAVID SHAPIRO WITH

GINI ALHADEFF

Ero in pace ed eccomi dannata
al sospetto che forse sono amata.

I was at peace and now I'm doomed
because I suspect that love has bloomed.

MOIRA EGAN AND

DAMIANO ABENI

Amore semplicissimo che crede alle parole,
poiché non posso fare quello che voglio fare
non ti posso abbracciare né baciare
il mio piacere è nelle mie parole
e quando posso ti parlo d'amore.
Così seduta davanti a un bicchiere
in un posto pieno di persone
se la tua fronte si increspa veloce
io parlo ad alta voce nell'ardore
tu non mi dici fa meno rumore
che ognuno pensi pure quel che vuole
io mi avvicino sciolta di languore
e tu negli occhi hai un tenero velame
io non ti tocco, neanche ti sfioro
ma nel tuo corpo mi sembra di nuotare,
e il divano di quel bar salotto
quando ci alziamo sembra un letto sfatto.

Very simple love that believes in words,
since I cannot do what I want to do,
can neither hug nor kiss you,
my pleasure lies in my words
and when I can I speak to you of love.
So, sitting with a drink in front of me,
the place filled with people,
if your forehead quickly creases
in the heat of the moment I speak too loudly
and you never say don't be so loud,
let them think whatever they want
I draw closer melting with languor
and your eyes are so sweetly veiled
I don't reach for you, no, not even the softest touch
but in your body I feel I am swimming,
and the couch in the bar's lounge
when we get up looks like an unmade bed.

J. D. MCCLATCHY

È tutto così semplice, sì, era così semplice,
è tale l'evidenza che quasi non ci credo.
A questo serve il corpo: mi tocchi o non mi tocchi,
mi abbracci o mi allontani. Il resto è per i pazzi.

It's all so simple, yes, it was so simple,
it is so clear I almost can't believe it.
Here's what the body is for: you touch me or you don't touch me,
you hold me or send me away. The rest is for lunatics.

GINI ALHADEFF

Tu mi vorresti come uno dei tuoi gatti
castrati e paralleli: dormono in fila infatti
e fanno i gatti solo di nascosto
quando non li vedi. Ma io non sarò mai
castrata e parallela. Magari me ne vado,
ma tutta di traverso e tutta intera.

You want me to be like one of your cats
castrated and parallel: they sleep in a row, as you know,
and are only cats offstage
when you don't see them. But I'll never be
castrated and parallel. I may leave,
but if I do it'll be sideways and in one piece.

GINI ALHADEFF

Non è stupefacente che una sera
mettendo dentro il suo sacchetto il pane
io ricominci il solito dettato,
riapra il repertorio, alzi il sipario
mostrando il tempo fermo, mai passato?
Niente è passato, non c'è più il passato,
l'attore nato non scorda mai la parte.

Isn't it amazing that one evening
sliding the bread into its paper sack
I start all over with the same old speech,
reopen the repertory, raise the curtain
to find time standing still, not ever passing?
Nothing has passed, the past doesn't exist,
born actors never do forget their parts.

GEOFFREY BROCK

Eccola trasformata in caramella
una caramella grande e ovale,
non in offerta, ma rigirata in bocca,
che lei da sola tutta se la succhia.

There she is turned into a lollipop
a large egg-shaped lollipop,
not passed around, but twirled in the mouth,
that she sucks on all by herself.

GINI ALHADEFF

Che poco mondo è il mio che è sempre nel bisogno
di te che pure con il tuo poco o niente
che hai da offrire non mi offriresti niente!
Perché ti cerco sempre, perché voglio vederti
se nel vederti vedo come è fatta
la mia sconfitta che è lì sulla tua faccia?

Sguardo velato non certo dal languore
ma lontananza tiepida e distratta,
bocca socchiusa non per lo stupore
ma solo noncuranza che la fiacca.

Un dopoguerra spento disarmato
un campo senza polvere o macerie
senza fuochi segreti e senza fumi,
piatta immobilità dove mi arrendo
dove anche la memoria si è sfinita.
Eppure come in ogni dopoguerra
si vuol ricostruire, ci si affanna.

What a meager world is mine that always needs you,
who even with the little or nothing
you have to offer would offer me nothing!
Why do I look for you always, why do I want to see you
if when I see you I see what
my defeat looks like, right there on your face?

A gaze veiled surely not by languor
but distance tepid and distracted,
the lips aren't parted out of wonder
thoughtlessness made them slack.

A postwar stilled and disarmed
a field without dust or rubble
without secret fires or smoke,
flat immobility where I surrender
where even memory played itself out.
And yet as in every postwar
there's the drive to rebuild, a rush to.

GINI ALHADEFF

No, io non posso amare quel che sei,
quello che sei è in verità uno sbaglio.
C'è in te però una grazia che oltrepassa
quello che tu in ostinatezza sei.
Qualche cosa che è tuo e non ti appartiene,
che è in te in origine ma da te diviso,
che a te si accosta cauto, spaventato
del suo stesso incontenibile splendore.

I cannot love what you are, no,
what you are is indeed a mistake.
But there is in you a grace that surpasses
what you obstinately are.
Something that's yours and doesn't belong to you,
in you from the start but separate from you,
that draws towards you cautiously, afraid
of its own uncontainable splendor.

GINI ALHADEFF

Sì sì, come l'altr'anno, tra il ventitré
e il ventiquattro giugno, quando sentivo il cuore
crescermi e irradiarsi, cuore in solstizio,
in espansione massima di luce.
Tutti quei raggi allora—ricordo che mangiavo
ciliegie enormi e quasi troppo dolci—
avevano un approdo, anche se lontanissimo
e insicuro. Ma adesso cosa mi invento
per questo cuore che si ripete
così ubbidiente alla stagione,
dove lo mando adesso, in quale vuoto?

Just like last year, yes, between the twenty-third
and twenty-fourth of June, when I felt my heart
grow in me and glow, heart in solstice,
in maximum expansion of light.
All those rays then—I remember I was eating
huge cherries that were almost too sweet—
had a mooring, though distant
and uncertain. What will I invent now
for this repeating heart
obeying seasons,
where will I send it now, into what void?

GINI ALHADEFF

Mi sembra di volere, ma che cos'è che voglio?
Desidero che cosa? Non lo so.
È come quando d'estate alzando gli occhi
al cielo sperando di vedere una stella
che cade, o che potrebbe cadere, incerta
dei miei voti mi affido pigra a quell'ambigua
parte di me segreta, separata da me,
da me dimenticata nel mio retrobottega
che forse tiene ancora in sé, se c'è,
la forma originale, lo stampo del piacere
e a voce chiusa dico: si compia ciò che voglio
si avveri il desiderio. Anche se non lo so
non lo conosco, la stella lei lo sa,
perché è lontana.

I think I want, but what is it I want?
Do I want something? I don't know.
It's like in the summer when lifting the eyes
to heaven, hoping to see a star
fall, or one that might fall, uncertain
of my vows I entrust myself lazily to that ambiguous
secret part of me, separate from me,
by me forgotten in some back room
which may still hold within it, if it's there,
its original shape, the mold of pleasure,
and with muted voice I say: may what I want come about
may the wish come true. Even though I don't know
don't know what that is, the star will know,
because it's far away.

GINI ALHADEFF

about the translators

DAMIANO ABENI is an Italian epidemiologist who, since 1973, has been translating American poets such as Ashbery, Bidart, Bishop, Ferlinghetti, Ginsberg, Strand, Simic, C. K. Williams, and others. With Mark Strand, he edited *West of Your Cities* (2003), a bilingual anthology of contemporary American poetry. He has held fellowships at the Liguria Study Center of the Bogliasco Foundation and the Rockefeller Foundation Bellagio Center, and he was a Director's Guest at the Civitella Ranieri Foundation.

BRUNELLA ANTOMARINI teaches aesthetics at John Cabot University in Rome. Her books include *Thinking Through Error* (2012), and her translations include Paul Vangelisti's *La vita semplice* (The Simple Life, 2009). She also edits *InVerse*, a yearly anthology of Italian poetry in English translation.

JUDITH BAUMEL is the author of three books of poetry: *The Weight of Numbers* (1988), which won the Walt Whitman Award; *Now* (1996); and *The Kangaroo Girl* (2011). A graduate of Radcliffe and Johns Hopkins, she teaches at Adelphi University and lives in the Bronx, where she was born.

GEOFFREY BROCK, born in Atlanta, is the author of *Weighing Light: Poems* (2005). His translations include Cesare Pavese's *Disaffections: Complete Poems 1930–1950* (2002) and he is the editor of *The FSG Book of Twentieth-Century Italian Poetry* (2012). His awards include the PEN USA Prize, the John Frederick Nims Memorial Prize, an NEA Literature Fellowship in poetry, and a Guggenheim Fellowship. He teaches at the University of Arkansas.

MOIRA EGAN is the author of *Cleave* (2004), *La Seta della Cravatta / The Silk of the Tie* (2009), *Bar Napkin Sonnets* (2009), and *Spin* (2010). With Damiano Abeni, she has published Italian translations of Ashbery, Barth,

Bender, Strand, and others. She has been a Mid Atlantic Arts Foundation Fellow at the Virginia Center for the Creative Arts, a Writer in Residence at the St. James Cavalier Centre for Creativity in Malta, a Fellow at the Civitella Ranieri Foundation, and a Fellow at the Rockefeller Foundation Bellagio Center.

JONATHAN GALASSI is an American poet, translator, and editor. His translations include Montale's *Collected Poems: 1920–1954* (1998) and Leopardi's *Canti* (2010); his own collections include *North Street* (2000) and *Left-handed* (2012). A former poetry editor of *The Paris Review*, he is president and publisher of Farrar, Straus and Giroux.

JORIE GRAHAM replaced poet Seamus Heaney as Boylston Professor at Harvard, becoming the first woman to be appointed to this position. She won the Pulitzer Prize for Poetry (1996) for *The Dream of the Unified Field: Selected Poems 1974–1994* and was chancellor of the Academy of American Poets from 1997 to 2003. She is the author of numerous collections of poetry, including her most recent, *Sea Change* (2008). She has also edited two anthologies, *Earth Took of Earth: 100 Great Poems of the English Language* (1996) and *The Best American Poetry 1990*. Graham's many honors include a John D. and Catherine T. MacArthur Fellowship and the Morton Dauwen Zabel Award from the American Academy and Institute of Arts and Letters.

KENNETH KOCH was a poet, playwright, and professor, active from the 1950s until his death in 2002. He was a prominent poet of the New York School, a loose group of poets including Frank O'Hara, John Ashbery, and David Shapiro, that eschewed contemporary introspective poetry in favor of an exuberant, cosmopolitan style that was mainly inspired by travel, painting, and music. His numerous honors included the Rebekah Johnson Bobbitt National Prize for Poetry, awarded by the Library of Congress in 1996, as well as awards from the American Academy of Arts and Letters and the Fulbright, Guggenheim, and Ingram Merrill foundations. In 1996 he was inducted as a member of the American Academy of Arts and Letters. Kenneth Koch lived in New York City, where he was professor of English at Columbia University.

J. D. MCCLATCHY is the author of six books of poems, three of prose, and fifteen opera libretti. In addition, he has edited dozens of books, including *The Vintage Book of Contemporary World Poetry*. He teaches at Yale, where he also serves as editor of *The Yale Review*.

DAVID SHAPIRO has written over twenty books of poetry (*After a Lost Original* and *A Burning Interior* among them) and criticism. In 1971, he was the youngest poet to be nominated for the National Book Award. He wrote the first monograph on John Ashbery, the first study of Mondrian's flowers, and the first book on Jasper Johns's drawings. Among his many awards and grants are the Morton Dauwen Zabel Award from the American Academy of Arts and Letters and a Foundation for Contemporary Arts Grants to Artists Award in 1996. A professional violinist in his youth, he is collaborating with the Anglo-Arab composer Mohammed Fairouz.

SUSAN STEWART is a poet, translator, and critic. She is the author, most recently, of the poetry books *Columbarium*, which won the National Book Critics Circle Award, and *Red Rover*, and of a book of prose, *The Poet's Freedom: A Notebook on Making*. A former MacArthur Fellow, she is the Avalon Foundation University Professor in the Humanities at Princeton University.

MARK STRAND is the author of numerous collections of poetry, including *Almost Invisible: Poems* (2012), *Man and Camel* (2006), and *Blizzard of One* (1998), which won the Pulitzer Prize. He has also written two books of prose, including *Hopper*, several volumes of translations, several monographs on contemporary artists, and three books for children. His honors include the Bollingen Prize, the Wallace Stevens Prize, and fellowships from the MacArthur Foundation and the Ingram Merrill Foundation. He has served as Poet Laureate of the United States and won the Gold Medal for Poetry from the American Academy of Arts and Letters. He currently teaches English and Comparative Literature at Columbia University in New York and lives in Madrid, Spain, and in New York City.

ROSANNA WARREN teaches English and Comparative Literature at the University of Chicago. Her book of criticism, *Fables of the Self: Studies in Lyric Poetry*, came out in 2008. Her most recent books of poems are *Departure* (2003) and *Ghost in a Red Hat* (2011).

acknowledgments

Alba Clemente introduced me to Patrizia Cavalli in 2006 and that is why this book exists. Renata Sperandio invited Patrizia and me to read at the Istituto Italiano di Cultura in New York in 2009, and that is how I first tried out my translations of Patrizia's poems before an American audience. That reading established the fact that it was time for Patrizia's work to become better known in America. Mark Strand was the first to sit down and translate twelve of her poems. Jorie Graham's wonderful translations arrived by e-mail, as did Rosanna Warren's. I am grateful to them all—to Sandy McClatchy, David Shapiro, and Geoffrey Brock for their inspired translations—and to all the poets who through the years have translated Patrizia's work and published it in journals and magazines—Judith Baumel, Susan Stewart with Brunella Antomarini, and Moira Egan with Damiano Abeni. I am grateful to Jonathan Galassi for his masterly translations and for willing this book into print at FSG. My own translations are dedicated to the memory of Fernanda Pivano. My greatest support—philological and moral—has come from Francesco Pellizzi.

Patrizia Cavalli wishes to thank all the American friends who over the years have sustained her work—Diane Kelder, Mary Kaplan, Mark Strand, Maxine Groffsky—and, more recently, Eliza Griswold. She would also like to thank, "if the dead can be thanked," her friend Kenneth Koch, whom she saw often on his frequent visits to Rome. He had written a poem titled "Talking to Patrizia" after a long conversation about a young woman he was in love with at the time, in the course of which Patrizia had given him "technical advice on how to seduce her."

index of titles and first lines in italian

index of titles and
first lines in english

Grateful acknowledgment is made for permission to print the following previously published and unpublished poems:

"Together eternity and death threaten me"; "Before when you left you would always forget"; "Ah yes, to your misfortune"; and "Now that time seems all mine": translation copyright © 1998 by Judith Baumel. "The Moroccans with the carpets": translation copyright © 1998 by Kenneth Koch. Originally published in *My Poems Will Not Change the World* (Toronto: Exile Editions, 1998). Reprinted by permission of Exile Editions.

"Always wanting to understand. You can't"; "I comb my hair"; "But first we must free ourselves"; "If you knocked now on my door"; "To get out of prison do you really need"; and "Don't count on my imagination, no": translation copyright © 2012 by Geoffrey Brock. Originally published in *The Cincinnati Review* (Spring 2012). Reprinted by permission of Geoffrey Brock.

"I'm going, but where? Oh gods!": translation copyright © 2013 by Geoffrey Brock. Originally published in *The American Reader* (Spring 2013). Reprinted by permission of Geoffrey Brock.

"To look at beauty and never make it yours"; "The streets are hot, the voices in the way"; and "Isn't it amazing that one evening": translation copyright © 2013 by Geoffrey Brock. Printed by permission.

"Love not mine not yours"; "So, let's see how you flower"; and "I was at peace and now I'm doomed": translation copyright © 2013 by Moira Egan and Damiano Abeni. Printed by permission.

"You arrive like this, as always"; "The Atlantic Day"; "Chair, stop being such a chair!"; "Now it's sure, the world doesn't exist"; "At first the little thought was easy"; "But those kids with twisted legs"; "Stopping suddenly, no destination"; "Fresco of the underwater night"; "How sweet it was yesterday imagining I was a tree!"; "The season is inviting me. Which season is"; "These lovely sheaves of poetry I find"; and "Surely it's ridiculous, maybe even scandalous": translation copyright © 2013 by Jonathan Galassi. Printed by permission.

"When one finds one's self unexpectedly selected by health"; "The body was a sheet it laid itself out"; "Again it has prepared itself for my awakening"; "Now

Grateful acknowledgment is made to the following publications, in which some of these poems first appeared:

Harper's Magazine: "Pockets," translated by Gini Alhadeff.

The Nation: "Eating a Macintosh apple," translated by David Shapiro with Gini Alhadeff; and "Two hours ago I fell in love," translated by Mark Strand.

The New Republic: "Therapy," translated by Mark Strand.

The Paris Review: "You sit at the head of the table," "When, thanks to the virtues of wine," "O really, she's with somebody?," and "In the seething almost Indian heat," translated by Mark Strand with Gini Alhadeff; "But you, are you Christians?," translated by Jorie Graham; "Surely it's ridiculous, maybe even scandalous," translated by Jonathan Galassi; "To look at beauty and never make it yours" and "Isn't it amazing that one evening," translated by Geoffrey Brock; "Very simple love that believes in words," translated by J. D. McClatchy; and "There she is turned into a lollipop," translated by Gini Alhadeff.

A Public Space: "Again it has prepared itself for my awakening," translated by Rosanna Warren.

Patrizia Cavalli was born in Todi, Umbria, and published her first collection of poems, *Le mie poesie non cambieranno il mondo*, in 1974. This is the first selection of her poems to appear in English since the 1998 Exile Editions volume published in Canada, *My Poems Will Not Change the World*. In Italy her readings attract high and enthusiastic attendance, and *Poesie* is in its sixteenth printing.

The long poem "La guardiana" included in that collection was also published in 2005 as a separate volume by Nottetempo, as was "La patria" (2011). Cavalli has translated Shakespeare's *The Tempest*, *Othello*, and *A Midsummer Night's Dream* in verse; Molière's *Amphytrion*; and Oscar Wilde's *Salomé*. Giulio Einaudi Editore has published *Le mie poesie non cambieranno il mondo* (1974); *Il cielo* (1981); *Poesie (1974–1992)*, the previous two titles reissued along with a collection of new poems (1992); *L'io singolare proprio mio* (1999); *Sempre aperto teatro* (1999); *Pigre divinità e pigra sorte* (2006); and *Tre risvegli* (2013). In addition to poetry, Patrizia Cavalli has written several radio plays; *Sotto non c'è niente*, an essay on Frida Kahlo (2008); *Flighty Matters*, five poems and a story on six pieces of attire (2012); and *Al cuore fa bene far le scale*, a book of songs with a CD (2012). She was made Chevalier de l'Ordre des Arts et des Lettres by the French government in 2003, won many of Italy's most prestigious literary prizes, including the Viareggio and the Pasolini, and has lived in Rome since 1968.

Gini Alhadeff, who published a memoir, *The Sun at Midday, Tales of a Mediterranean Family*, and a novel, *Diary of a Djinn*, was born of Italian parents in Alexandria, Egypt, where Italian and French were spoken at home, and learned English at the age of ten when her family moved to Japan. She started translating at the age of sixteen, from English into Italian, and later from Italian and French into English. In Manhattan, in the late 1980s to the early '90s, she founded and edited two literary quarterlies, *Normal* and *XX!st Century*, publishing many poets (Adonis, Irina Ratushinskaya, Victor Segalen) and writers (E. M. Cioran, Aldo Busi, Anna Maria Ortese) in translation. She is completing a new book, *The Magic Horn*, the story of a Swiss-American psychiatrist who started a garden at Bellevue Hospital in New York and filled it with concrete sculptures she built with her patients.